American Horses

RALPH MOODY

Illustrated by Neil O'Keeffe

University of Nebraska Press
Lincoln and London

First Nebraska paperback printing: 2004

Library of Congress Cataloging-in-Publication Data
Moody, Ralph, 1898–
American horses / Ralph Moody; illustrated by Neil O'Keeffe.
p.   cm.
Includes bibliographical references (p.   ).
ISBN 0-8032-8301-6 (pbk.: alk. paper)—ISBN 0-8032-3248-9
(hardcover: alk. paper)
1. Horses—United States—History—Juvenile literature.
2. Horses—Breeding—United States—History—Juvenile literature.
I. O'Keeffe, Neil, ill.   II. Title.
SF302.M65   2004
636.1'00973—dc22
2004004968

This Bison Books edition follows the original in beginning chapter 1 on
arabic page 11; the text remains unaltered.

CONTENTS

American Horses

1

The First American Horse

IT IS little wonder that we Americans are horse lovers, for this is the homeland of the horse. Horses lived here, but nowhere else on earth, for more than fifty million years before the Indians came. Then they all left this continent as mysteriously as if they had followed a Pied Piper away, never to return until they were brought back by the Spanish conquistadors and early European colonists.

Through fossil discoveries the history of the horse can be traced more accurately than that of any other creature on earth. It shows him to have been one of the most adaptable of all creatures, capable of making physical adjustments to meet the changing conditions under which he must live. The first known member of the horse family was a timid little animal no larger than a small sheep, with three toes on his hind feet and four on his front feet. This continent was then low and marshy, so these little ancestors of the horse fed on the lush plants that grew along the water edge, and hid among them to escape their enemies.

Then, as ages passed, the water receded, the land rose, and the little horses were forced to find their living on solid ground, quite possibly rolling prairies. But as the land changed, the horse gradually evolved to meet the new conditions. He needed more and larger teeth for grinding hard grass, so his head grew larger to make room for them, and his body grew in proportion to his head. Without horns or fangs for fighting his enemies, and being too big to hide from them, he needed speed with which to escape them, so his legs grew long and his running muscles strong. To gain greater speed he ran on one tiptoe of each foot, so the claw on that toe grew into a solid hoof that was large enough to support the weight of the body, and the unused toes disappeared.

Except for the eruptions that threw up some of our mountains, the changes that took place in the formation of the land on this continent were so gradual as to be almost unnoticeable from century to century. Except for the birth of mutants — almost as rare as eruptions in the surface of the earth — the changes which took place in the development of the horse from generation to generation were equally gradual, for offspring inherit the physical and mental characteristics of their parents and recent ancestors. A mutant is an offspring quite unlike either of his parents or any of his recent ancestors.

The study of fossils not only tells the story of the horse's fifty-million-year evolution on this continent, but of his travels throughout the world. After horses had developed until they were nearly like those of the present age they became great travelers, roaming from the tip of South America nearly to the Arctic Circle. Then, for some reason not yet known, they left this continent, crossed the land bridge that then existed between Alaska and Siberia, and spread throughout Asia, Europe, and Africa. And wherever they went, they evolved to suit the region in which they made their new homes.

Those that turned south into China became shaggy, docile ponies. Those that made their new home on the steppes of Russia, where feed was

scarce and the winters cold, grew heavy coats and became chunky, but remained small. In the lowlands of western Europe, where feed was abundant and the weather temperate, the horse more than doubled his size, and became a coarse-boned, plodding animal. In the mountainous parts of France and Spain he learned to change his traveling gait from the trot to the pace. For, when going down steep hills, a horse can balance himself better if both legs on either side are moved forward at the same time. The greatest refinement of the horse took place in the desert countries surrounding

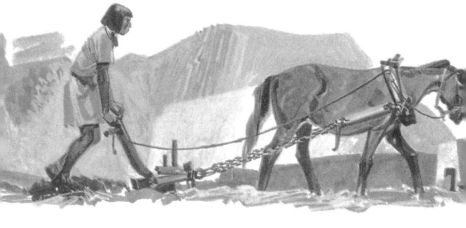

the eastern end of the Mediterranean Sea. In this hot, dry region he had to travel great distances to find feed and water. His bones became more hard and slender, his coat thinner and silkier, his speed and courage developed remarkably, and he acquired tremendous endurance.

It is probable that the horse and the dog were the first wild creatures domesticated, and it is certain that the horse has had a greater influence on the lives of men than any other animal. Through use of the horse man first became able to travel great distances swiftly, and to kill fast-running game with

his primitive weapons. But the horse's greatest value to ancient man was in battle, for it was soon discovered that warriors mounted on horses could easily overcome an enemy who lacked them.

No one knows when horses were first domesticated, but it was probably more than five thousand years ago. From Biblical history we know that more than four thousand years ago the Assyrians used war horses in their battles against the Babylonians. By the time of Alexander the Great, horses were being used throughout the then known world for war, transportation, and burden bearing. The tribes or nations having the best horses prospered and won their battles; those with the poorest lost and were conquered.

With horses playing so important a part in the lives of men it was only natural that men should strive to improve their stock, each nation trying to develop a horse best suited to the needs of its people, both in their daily lives and in warfare. The Arabs were by far the most successful of these early horsemen. By using the native horse of the deserts, and by mating the best with the best for hundreds of generations, they developed a horse that was matchless for desert transportation and warfare. Although small, fine-boned, exquisitely beautiful, and gentle, the Arabian horses had amazing speed, tremendous endurance, and boundless courage in battle. Through raids and trading, the Berbers, Turks, and other desert people acquired Arabian stallions and improved their own horses until, though not so beautiful, they had nearly the speed and endurance of the Arabians'. Then the Berbers conquered Spain, mated their war horses with the native stock, and produced the ancestors of our western mustangs.

In France the pacing horses were developed into saddle mounts having a comfortable ambling gait, and in the rich lowlands of western Europe the ponderous, coarse-boned horses were trained for farm work. England had no native horses, for, being an island, the wild herds could not reach it. But long before the recording of English history, horses had been imported from the mainland, most of them the small, easy-gaited, ambling saddle horses of France. These were of little use to the English as war horses, for a knight in full armor weighed nearly four hundred pounds. To carry so heavy a

load the largest horses to be found in the Low Countries were imported, and the Great Horse of England was developed. Through the power of their thunderous charges the English knight and his Great Horse were invincible in battle until they were pitted against Turkish cavalry. Then they were a complete failure. The Turks, excellent horsemen and mounted on small, swift desert horses, harried them as a collie dog harries a bull. Avoiding their overpowering charges, the Turks circled them, darted in from behind, and cut down the slow and ponderous horses of the knights as if they had been oxen.

The failure of the Great Horse against the small, swift horses of the deserts eventually resulted in the development of the fastest race horse on earth. In the early 1700's the British set about to produce a cavalry horse that would be somewhat larger than the Arabian, but which would retain all of the desert horse's speed and endurance. To accomplish this, three exceptionally fine desert stallions were imported and mated with the best English mares. They were the Byerly Turk, the Darley Arabian, and the Godolphin Barb — the horse of the Berbers. It was soon discovered that the offspring of these three great sires were faster runners than the desert horses themselves — and wherever there are men and fast horses there is bound to be racing. By carefully selected matings over a period of a hundred years, a new and superior breed of horse, the Thoroughbred, was perfected. All registered Thoroughbreds throughout the world are descendants of these three great desert stallions.

America has been called the melting pot of the world, for people of many races and nationalities have come here, intermarried, and produced a new people. It might also be called the melting pot of the horse world, for the pioneers from each nation brought with them the horses of their homeland. Here these horses have been intermated at random until most of them have entirely lost their original identity and are now of no particular breed or type. But out of the melting pot have come four entirely new breeds that rank among the finest horses of the world. Three of them originated through the painstaking and intelligent efforts of American horsemen, one through a freak of nature.

2

The Big Little Horse

No PEOPLE on earth owe the horse a greater debt than we Americans. Without his strength and obedience our early colonists could not have cleared the land and tilled the soil. Without his speed for carrying communications the colonies could not have been held together to win our independence. Without his stout legs and endurance our pioneers could not have settled the wilderness, crossed the deserts, and extended the boundaries of the United States from the Atlantic to the Pacific. And, until the development of the airplane and mobile unit, we could not have won our wars without the horse's strength, courage, and intelligence. But possibly our greatest debt is to a single horse: a little bay stallion born when George Washington was President.

At the end of the Revolutionary War most of the people of this new nation were farmers, living along the Atlantic Coast from Maine to Georgia. The Appalachian Mountains formed the frontier. To the westward remained a vast, unexplored wilderness. But the pioneer spirit was strong in the early Americans. As good farms along the coast became scarce, frontiersmen pushed westward, following the rivers that flowed down from the mountains, and clearing new farms in the fertile valleys.

Washington had been President nearly three years before Vermont joined the Union. Because it was entirely covered by heavily forested mountains it was called the Green Mountain State, but along its river valleys the soil was rich and deep. Here fertile farms could be claimed from the wilderness, but only by pioneers who were as rugged as the mountains themselves, and only with the help of horses that were equally rugged.

Every acre of the Vermont farm land had to be cleared of logs, stumps, and boulders, and to do this, work horses of unusual strength were required. But strength alone was not enough. Until crops could be raised there was no hay or grain for horses, the settlements were far apart, and the roads between them were no more than wheel tracks through the forests. To prosper on this frontier the pioneers needed a horse with the strength and endurance to pull heavy loads from dawn till dusk, and with the hardiness to pick up its own living by grazing. It must be gentle enough to be handled by women and children, and have speed to get over the roads rapidly if a doctor were needed. But there had never been such horses. Those that were strong enough for the heavy work in the woods were too slow and clumsy to be good road horses. Those that were fast enough to be good driving horses were usually high-strung, nervous, and unfit for heavy work in the woods. Few horses of any type, if worked or driven, were hardy enough to rustle for their own living.

Next to an unshakable faith in God, the greatest need of the American pioneers was for a type of horse such as had never been known; one that was as hardy and rugged as they themselves, and that could fill their every requirement for strength, en-

durance, and speed. Nature met the need by producing a mutant: a horse that was unlike his parents
or any other horse ever known.

At the time the Declaration of Independence was
signed, Justin Morgan lived on a small farm near
West Springfield, Massachusetts. He was not
strong enough to do heavy farm work, but was better
educated than most of his neighbors, and had a fairly
good singing voice. Because of his love of horses
he lived on a farm, and kept a fine driving mare, but
because of his poor health he made his living by
teaching school and driving about the country to
give singing lessons.

In spite of his health, Justin Morgan was a pioneer
by nature. When Springfield began growing into
a city he decided to move his family farther into the
frontier. Soon after Washington was inaugurated
President, Mr. Morgan sold his farm at West Springfield to his cousin Abner. And, since Abner had
very little money, it was agreed that the farm should
be paid for over a number of years.

As soon as the sale had been made, Justin Morgan
loaded his few articles of furniture and his family
onto a wagon, and started northward along the

Connecticut River Valley. He followed the river more than two hundred miles to the north, then turned westward along the White River. Far up the valley, in the heart of the Green Mountains, he reached the little clearing of Randolph and settled there. Not being strong enough to clear land for farming, he opened a little tavern and taught school.

When Vermont became a state of the Union, the little settlement of Randolph began to grow and Justin Morgan prospered, but he was worried about the money due him on the farm he had sold to his cousin Abner. Three years had passed, and he had received no payment, so when fall came he drove back to West Springfield to collect. Times had not been good in southern Massachusetts, and Abner still had no money. As part payment on his debt he offered to turn over to Mr. Morgan a three-year-old gelding that had been halter-broken, and a chunky two-year-old bay colt that was the gelding's playmate.

Justin Morgan had no need for horses himself and little interest in the unbroken colt, but horses were badly needed in the Green Mountains, and he was sure he could find a market there for the gelding.

Although he would much rather have had a payment of fifty dollars, he tied the gelding to the seat of his road cart and drove away on his two-hundred-and-fifty-mile trip back to Randolph. The chunky little bay colt trailed along behind, stopping now and again to nibble a few mouthfuls of grass, but always catching up again.

Back in Randolph Mr. Morgan had no trouble in selling the gelding, but no one wanted to buy the bay colt. In the first place, he was unbroken and too young to be worked. And in the second place, the little fellow didn't look as though he'd

ever amount to much. Anyone could see that he was too small to make much of a work horse, and he was too chunky to be a good riding or driving horse. Besides that, he was a peculiar-looking animal, with too much body for his short legs. One man who came to look at him shook his head and said, "No, siree, I wouldn't have no use for a critter the likes o' that one. Never seen a hoss with a more unlikely figger." That was enough to mark the little bay colt. Within a few days everyone in Randolph was calling him "Figure."

Few colts are kept entire unless of such outstand-

ing quality as to become fine sires, for stallions are often unruly and dangerous. But Figure was as gentle and friendly as a kitten, so Justin Morgan neglected having him gelded. The children could pet him, and even climb on his back, though he was not yet halter-broken. It might also have seemed that Figure knew he was being laughed at for his small size and stubby legs, and that he was trying to make himself look bigger. He arched his heavy neck, carried his head proudly, lifted his feet high, and looked as if he were strutting when he walked or trotted.

Justin Morgan was busy with his teaching and his tavern, and paid little attention to the colt he had taken in as part payment on a bad debt. During the fall Figure wandered around the settlement as he pleased, grazing wherever he found grass. When the long Vermont winter set in with subzero weather and deep snows, he found shelter in the woods, pawing through the snow for the dried grass that lay beneath.

Although the Vermont pioneers kept their stock in barns during the winter, feed was scarce, and by springtime most of their horses were thin and bony.

But Figure, living in the open and rustling for his feed, had come through in fine shape, and had reached his full size. Though only fourteen hands (fifty-six inches) at the withers, he held his head higher than horses that were six or eight inches taller. The muscles of his shoulders and thighs were thick and bulging, his short back was coupled by stout loins to his level-crouped hindquarters, his ribs were widesprung, and he was deep in the chest. But with it all, he weighed less than nine hundred pounds, and no one wanted to buy him.

Randolph, like most frontier settlements, had its town ne'er-do-well. Bob Evans was a happy-go-lucky fellow and a hard worker, but he never got ahead. Although Bob was no drunkard, he had a taste for rum, and by the time he had his tavern bill paid, there was never anything left with which to buy a horse. The spring that Figure turned three years old, Bob got the job of clearing a fifteen-acre farm for one of his neighbors. The land was covered by a heavy stand of pine and dotted with great boulders. To clear it would be a two-year job for a man with a good team of horses. But all Bob had was his own strong back, a love and understanding of horses, and an overdue tavern bill. He did the best he could under the circumstances, but no one in Randolph thought his best was very good; he hired Figure from Justin Morgan for fifteen dollars a year, promising to pay two dollars of the hire whenever he had cleared an acre.

To harness-break a three-year-old stallion that has never worn a halter, and has run wild in the woods all winter, is no task for an ordinary man. But Bob Evans was no ordinary man, and Figure was no ordinary stallion. From the beginning Bob had affection for the little bay horse that nobody wanted, and Figure had affection for Bob Evans. There was never any breaking to it; it was simply a matter of Bob teaching Figure what was wanted of him, and Figure doing his level best to please the man who understood and was good to him. From dawn till dusk the man and the little bay stallion worked as partners in the woods — dragging out logs for the sawmill, pulling stumps, and hauling boulders to fill the swamps. When evening came Bob vaulted onto Figure's back, rode him to the settlement, and turned him loose to graze.

Randolph was a typical backwoods settlement of

the late 1700's. Its single street ran along the river-bank, where the land was level. On the river side of the street was the sawmill, where logs could be hauled from the back country or floated downstream in rafts. Below it, with its paddle wheel turned by the river, was the gristmill, and across the street were the general store, the blacksmith's shop, and the tavern. Farther down the street the spire of the church stood white against the dark green of the pine-covered hills. In its shadow stood the log schoolhouse, where Justin Morgan taught the pioneers' children while his wife tended bar in the tavern. And, as in all frontier settlements, the social life of the country roundabout centered in the church and the tavern.

Vermont pioneers were hard-working, religious men. No Sunday passed without their coming to "meeting" at the church — and no load of logs was hauled to the sawmill without their stopping at the tavern to "wet their whistle with a dollop o' rum," to visit with any other frontiersmen who might happen to be in town, and maybe to make a wager on whose horse could pull the most or run the fastest.

September was nearly gone and early dusk was settling when Bob Evans unhitched Figure from the last log of the day, looped the traces of the harness over the hame posts, and climbed wearily to the little horse's back. It had been a hard day, but the little bay stallion held his head proudly as he trotted off toward the settlement. The dusk had nearly turned to darkness when Bob rode Figure into sight of Randolph. They were nearing the schoolhouse when Nathan Nye came running to meet them.

"By gorry, Bob, you missed the fun!" he shouted as he came closer. "You see that all-fired big log yonder? There's been half a dozen hosses tried to drag it up to the sawmill this afternoon, and couldn't a one of 'em budge it. None 'ceptin' that big geldin' o' Lisha Shaply's, and he wa'n't able to move it more'n two foot. Over to the tavern they're offerin' to bet a gallon o' rum there ain't a hoss in these parts can drag that there log to the mill in three starts."

Bob slid from Figure's back and walked across the road to look at the log more closely. It certainly was a big one, but the pull to the sawmill would be over level ground, and Bob knew Figure had pulled heavier logs than that in the woods. If it were morning he'd have little doubt of Figure's ability to drag the log as far as the sawmill — but they'd had a hard day in the woods, and no horse could be expected to pull his best when he was tired. Besides that, a whole gallon of rum would cost nearly as much as Bob could earn in a week and, if he should lose, his wife would give him fits. He'd have to do a little thinking about it before running so big a risk.

They were no sooner inside the tavern than Nye shouted, "Bob here, he allows his hoss could, like as not, drag that pine log over to the sawmill yard in three starts."

"His hoss?" someone bellowed. "You don't mean that runty bay colt o' Justin Morgan's? That ain't no hoss; that's only an overgrowed pony."

As the crowd hooted and laughed, someone else shouted, "I don't doubt me he could haul it, Bob, if you was to saw it into three pieces, but that wa'n't what we was betting on. We was betting on haulin' it in three starts, not three pieces."

Having his friends laugh at Figure made Bob

Evans angry. He banged a fist down on the bar and shouted back at them, "Why, I'd be ashamed to hitch my hoss onto a little log the likes o' that one! But I'll tell ye what I'll do, by gorry! If three of ye'll git on it and ride, I'll bet a gallon o' rum my hoss can drag it clean into the sawmill yard in two starts, 'stead o' three! Nathan, you go fetch a lantern and a log chain, and hunt up a good stout whiffletree!"

Laughing and hooting, the men trooped out of the tavern and down the street, Nathan Nye carrying the lantern and leading the way. Bob Evans

was doing no laughing. He was, first and last, a horseman, and he was still angry at these men who were making fun of Figure. Without a word he led the little horse into position at the end of the log. He would let no one help with the chain, but fastened it carefully, so the pull would be straight-away and slightly upward. When he had hooked the traces to the singletree he went to Figure's head, patted his neck, and ran a hand under the collar to be sure there was no wrinkle against his shoulder. Then he led him forward, just enough to tighten the chain and give him a feel of the load.

With the three heaviest men seated on the log, Bob took his place to the left of Figure's rump, picked up the reins, drew them snug, and clucked quietly. The little horse leaned into the collar, planted both hind feet evenly and wide apart, then arched his neck and squatted low on his haunches as he gathered the powerful muscles of his thighs. For a bare instant he relaxed the tension on the traces, then drove his shoulders into the collar with every muscle of his body tensed to the utmost and in perfect coordination.

As the chain links creaked and groaned at the strain, the tendons of Figure's cannons and gaskins vibrated like taut steel cables, the contracting muscles under his glossy hide corded and rippled. With his hind feet planted squarely, he heaved his shoulders to the left, then to the right, breaking the log loose from its bed and inching it forward. As the great log yielded grudgingly to the steady pull, Figure shot one hind foot forward a few inches for a better purchase on the ground, then the other. With each inch gained the log moved a bit less slowly, and the little horse quickened his steps.

Before half the distance to the sawmill had been

covered Figure's legs were working like the pistons of a racing engine, and Bob Evans was having to run to keep up with him. With the halfway mark well past, Bob stopped him for a short breather. Then the little stallion bowed his neck again, bunched his muscles, and in his second start dragged the great log with its load of astonished men to the sawmill yard. History doesn't tell us what happened to the gallon of rum, but it was doubtlessly toasted to the "biggest little horse" in the Green Mountains.

3

Figure

DURING THE LATE 1700's entertainment was scarce in the backwoods and, unless the weather was too bad, the pioneers worked from daybreak until darkness. But Fair Day was the exception, and every frontier family looked forward to it. When the crops had been gathered in, the winter's wood stacked in the woodshed, the pork barrel filled, and the windowpanes began frosting over at night, it was fair time. Men sorted out their largest ears of corn, laid aside the biggest pumpkin, and fed their best horse grain so he'd be in fine shape for the pulling contests or races. Women hurried to finish a patchwork quilt for the exhibits, the older girls set aside their clearest glasses of wild-currant jelly, and the boys tried to teach their dogs new tricks.

Fair Day in Randolph was in late October. By

FIGURE | 39

an hour after sunrise farm wagons were rolling into the settlement from as far as fifty miles away. Long before noon dozens of wagons stood along the river-bank and in the clearings around the buildings of the settlement. Nearly a hundred horses were tied to the wagons, nibbling hay from the boxes, or neighing and pawing the ground nervously. Cattle lowed, sheep bleated, and pigs squealed as the judges passed among them, choosing the best of each kind. While the women exhibited their handi-work at the church, the farmers were equally busy at the gristmill, polishing and laying out the best samples from their year's crop for the inspection of the judges.

Before the picnic baskets were opened the fron-tiersmen gathered at the tavern, visiting with neigh-bors, and wagering with each other on the sports of the afternoon. There would be logrolling at the millpond; rail-splitting, log-sawing, and wood-chopping contests at the sawmill. There would be stump-pulling contests for the strongest horses, and quarter-mile walking, trotting, and running races for the fastest. Most of the men bet on their own ability, or on the strength or speed of their own horses.

None of the wagers was large, and none of them in money. There would be a plug of tobacco here, a gallon of rum there; a bushel of potatoes, a lamb, or a pig.

Bob Evans had no crops to exhibit, so he and Figure worked in the woods during the morning, but at noon Bob rode him into Randolph. He joined his friends at the tavern and offered to bet a plug of tobacco against a bushel of potatoes that Figure could outpull any horse at the fair. Those who had seen the little bay stallion drag the big log to the sawmill yard kept quiet. But those who had not heard of it laughed derisively. Every one of them wanted to take Bob's bet, but, as always, he was broke and could wager no more than one plug of tobacco.

As the rum jug passed from hand to hand the frontiersmen grew louder in boasting of the speed or strength of their own horses, as well as louder in their ridicule of the stubby-legged little stallion. Bob Evans was used to being laughed at for his failures, and could take it good-naturedly, but it made him angry to hear Figure ridiculed. When the hooting was at its height he shouted, "I'll bet

FIGURE | 41

the clearin' of an acre o' land agin five bushels o' corn that my little hoss can outpull, outwalk, out-trot, or outrun any hoss in the Green Mountains!"

Vermont frontiersmen were betting men, and there were few who were above cheating a bit in a horse trade, but they wouldn't rob a friend by taking so foolish a bet when he was angry. None of them could believe the little stallion had even an outside chance in any one of the contests. There were horses at the fair that outweighed him by five hundred pounds, and were famous for their pulling power. There were long-legged walkers that could cover a mile in slightly over six minutes, trotters that were known for their speed throughout the frontier, and fast gallopers that had been grain-fed, rested, and readied for the past month. The men slapped Bob on the back and gave him a drink from the jug, but no one of them would take his offer.

When the picnic baskets were empty and the lumberjacks' contests finished, the pulling horses were harnessed and led across the clearing to a stump field. Among them, Figure looked like a pony, but he held his head high, stepped proudly,

and pricked his ears forward at the rows of stumps.
Of course, he had no idea he was going to compete
against these big horses in a pulling contest, but
he had no need to know it. During the months he
had worked in the woods he had learned to consider
every stump his adversary, and Bob had taught him
the best way of making his attack.

The judge led the way to the edge of the clearing, and when the crowd had gathered in a wide
circle he shouted the rules of the contest. The first
trials would be made on stumps measuring sixteen
inches in diameter, and each horse would be given

FIGURE | 43

five minutes to tear one from the ground. Those that failed would be eliminated from the contest; those that succeeded would move on to larger stumps until the winner was determined. The horses would compete in order of their weight: the largest first, and the smallest last. Whips might be used, but not goads. And the gentlemen would please be careful of their language, remembering there were ladies and children present.

One after another the biggest horses were hitched to the first stump chosen by the judge, and made their pulls while their drivers shouted encouragement and flogged them with a whip. Some set their ponderous hoofs solidly in the half-frozen ground, and strained against the collar with every ounce of their strength until they had run out their time. Some horses balked and quit when they had made their best pull and the stump refused to budge. Now and again a driver seesawed his horse, pulling it in one direction, then another. Others started with a loose chain, and whipped their horses into repeated, yanking lunges, but still the stump stood solidly.

It seemed evident that, with the ground frozen

two or three inches deep, the judge had picked too stout a stump for a single horse to pull. He had already chosen a smaller one for the next round of trials, and the crowd was moving toward it when Bob Evans shouted, "Wait up there! I ain't had my chance at this one yet!"

The idea of Bob's thinking Figure might have a chance against a stump that the biggest horses in the mountains had been unable to budge amused the crowd, and it moved away laughing. Someone shouted back, "Better save that little hoss o' yourn for pullin' pussy willows, Bob! He wa'n't built for stumps!"

Bob paid no attention to the jeering crowd, but led Figure to the stump where the big horses had failed. He carefully bound the heavy chain high around the stump, where the pull would have the greatest leverage against the roots. After he had hooked the traces, he adjusted Figure's collar, led him a step forward to bring the chain snug, patted his neck a stroke or two, and with the reins still looped over the hame post, stepped aside.

This was a game that Figure knew well. He needed no reins to guide him, and no whip to urge

FIGURE | 45

him on. The moment Bob stepped away the little horse planted his hind feet solidly, wide apart, and well out behind him. The muscles rippled along his back and quarters as he bunched them for action. For the first time that afternoon his head came down, he bowed his neck, tucked his chin close in toward his breast, and with ears pricked sharply forward, stood waiting the command from his friend and master.

There was something about the action of the little stallion that stopped the jeering of the crowd like magic. Men, women, and children stood watching in dead silence, and for a moment Bob let them wait. Then he spoke sharply, "Hup, boy! Hit it!"

As though the voice had triggered an explosion, every muscle in Figure's body leaped into action. His ears pinned themselves tight to his neck, his solidly planted hoofs dug into the frozen ground, and his shoulders crashed against the collar like twin battering rams.

The instant the force of the drive was spent, Figure slacked off on the chain, stood with body relaxed, head up, and ears pricked for the next command. The crowd was so still that a squirrel in the woods might have been heard chattering as Bob let the little horse rest a few seconds, then commanded, "Gee off, Figger!"

With just enough pull on the chain to keep it free of the ground, Figure side-stepped to the right, circled a quarter of the distance around the stump, then set himself for another wrenching yank. Again he hurled every ounce of his strength against the collar, relaxed, and side-stepped at Bob's command.

After Figure's fourth wrenching pull he had completely circled the stump, but it stood as solidly as it had before he was hitched to it. On his fifth pull the earth cracked, and a great root sprang to the surface. On his sixth, two more roots tore loose. And on his seventh drive against the chain, there was a snapping and groaning as the great stump yielded an inch or two to the pull. Figure needed no command from Bob now. He had felt the give, and Bob had long since taught him how to take advantage of it.

This time there was no relaxing of his muscles. He eased the strain just enough to let the stump spring back, then drove his shoulders into the collar again. And again. And again. With each drive the

earth cracked in a wider circle, roots sprang like taut cables from the ground, and the stump rocked farther over on its side. As the crowd cheered and shouted, Figure ripped the last remaining roots from the earth, and stood relaxed and blowing, waiting for the feel of Bob's rewarding pat on his rump. There was no doubting which horse was the champion stump-puller in the Green Mountains. In less than four minutes Figure had ripped a stump from the earth that no other horse at the fair could budge an inch.

The men who had been loudest in ridiculing the little bay stallion were now the loudest in their praise. As Bob Evans unhooked the traces they crowded around to shake his hand, congratulate him on his training, and offer him a drink from the rum jug. That was probably the first time in his life that Bob Evans ever refused a free drink. He pushed the jug away and told his friends, "Nope! Nope! Got to keep m'self sober for ridin' my hoss in the races."

Again the crowd howled with laughter, and someone shouted, "You'd have a better chance if you done the runnin' yourself, Bob, and left that little

FIGURE | 49

hoss ride you; your legs is longer'n hisn."

Success and pride seemed to have gone to Bob's head, and the insult to Figure again made him angry. Raising his voice above the noise of the crowd, he shouted, "I got a bushel o' 'taters and a plug o' tobacca says my hoss can outwalk ary one ye fetched along! Now put up or shut up!"

There was no man at the fair but knew how badly Bob's family needed the bushel of potatoes he had won on the stump-pulling contest, and none would bet against it, but one stepped forward to wager a bushel of corn against a plug of tobacco that his horse could outwalk Figure.

The races were to be held on the stretch of road that ran along the river and through the settlement. Though level, the road was little more than a pair of deeply rutted wheel tracks with a horse path between them. All the horse races — walking, trotting, and running — were to be at a quarter of a mile, starting at a big pine tree at the edge of the clearing and ending in front of Justin Morgan's tavern. As in all frontier races, the horses would be ridden, even at the trot, for the roads were too narrow to allow carts or carriages to pass each other.

The horse races were the most popular events at all these early-day fairs. With the stump-pulling contest over, the people hurried back across the clearing — the women and children anxious to find places along the roadside where they would have a good view of the finish line, the men to exercise their fastest horses and get them ready for the races.

Bob Evans seemed to be in no hurry — and, certainly, after a half-day's work at stump-pulling, there was no reason for exercising Figure. Bob rode him to the tavern at a walk, unharnessed him, all except the bridle, and tied a piece of rope to the

bit rings to serve as reins. All about him tall horses were being saddled for the walking race, and light boys mounted, as their fathers gave them last-minute instructions. Bob had no saddle, but vaulted to Figure's back and jogged him away toward the starting line.

At the tall pine tree a dozen horses were lined up across the roadway, the favorites in the middle where the going was best, and those with less chance of winning toward the outside. Figure was given a place at the end of the line, far out in the tall grass of a meadow. The only rule of the race was that the gait must be a flat-footed walk; any horse jogging or trotting would be disqualified.

After the starter had given the rule he stood at the end of the line near Figure's head, slammed his hat to the ground, and shouted "Go!" All along the line boys kicked their heels, and the horses stepped quickly away from the line. Bob Evans held his rope reins snug, so that Figure might not break into a trot, leaned forward a trifle, and clucked gently. Within seconds the line had become wedge-shaped, the horses at the center well out in front of those in the grass at the roadside. Among the horses far out in the meadow, only Figure was keeping anywhere near abreast of the leaders. But the natural high action of his feet made the tall grass of little hindrance to him, and he moved with a free-swinging, easy gait.

Urging the little horse on with his knees, and holding the reins snug to keep him out of a trot, Bob angled in toward the wheel tracks. The angle was a big handicap, and by the time he and Figure reached the roadway, the long-stepping leaders were four or five lengths ahead of them. Figure had

FIGURE | 53

never before been in a race of any kind, but from the moment he came into the roadway it was evident that he sensed the competition. And it was even more evident that he was determined to win in spite of his handicap. With his ears pricked sharply toward the leaders, he arched his neck and lengthened his stride, but there was no nervous tightening of the muscles. Under his glistening hide his shoulders slid forward and back as loosely as those of a cat, and with each forward thrust his head bobbed up and down.

There was no doubt in Bob Evans' mind that Figure was gaining on the leaders, but the gain was not enough. Three lengths still separated him from a long-striding black and a chestnut, and a length in front of them a tall gray gelding glided along with a smooth seven-foot stride. Worse still, the gray's rider was a boy weighing less than eighty pounds, while Bob weighed more than twice that much. He shifted his weight well forward, making the load easier to carry and giving the little horse more freedom of action in his hindquarters. Instantly Figure responded to the shifting of the weight. His stride lengthened by inches, and his head bobbed faster as his hoofs beat a tattoo on the frozen ground.

At the halfway mark the gray gelding appeared to be the sure winner. Two lengths behind him the chestnut and black battled it out, shoulder to shoulder, in the wheel ruts. Figure's bobbing head was now close to their rumps, and he was coming on fast. But those rumps were less than two feet apart. If Bob were to pull out into the tall grass there would be little chance of passing, and if he should try to go through the middle he would almost surely

be squeezed and held back. Bob never had to make the decision; Figure made it for himself. With a surge of power he drove his shoulders into the narrow opening. The chestnut spooked and broke into a trot; the black side-stepped, lost stride, and fell back.

With only the gray in front of him, Figure buckled down to his task, his head bobbing like a busy woodpecker's. He was having to take five strides to the long-legged gelding's four, but he laid his ears tight back to his neck and his hoofs beat like sticks on a snare drum. And with each step he gained an inch or two on the gray.

At the schoolhouse Figure's shoulder was even with the gelding's hip, and he was still gaining an inch or two with every stride, but there were barely fifty yards left to the finish line. Both sides of the roadway were lined with men, women, and children — cheering on the little horse that wouldn't give up. And as if in answer to their cheers, Figure called on that extra reserve of drive that only a champion has. He crossed the finish line with his nose a scant six inches in front of the gray gelding's.

Trotting races were always the most popular with

the early New Englanders, for their need was for a horse that could pull a carriage rapidly over the rough roads. At the Randolph fair there were twenty horses entered for the trot. This was too many to be lined up for a single start, so it was decided to divide the horses and run them in two heats, with a third to be run off between the two winners.

As was customary, the horses with the greatest reputation for speed were placed in the first heat, and those which were thought to have little chance in the second. It was no surprise that Figure was placed in the second heat, but it had its advantages. It gave him a little time for rest after the walking race, and it gave Bob Evans a chance to make a few wagers at long odds.

From where Bob stood in front of the tavern it was hard to see the first half of the race, for the horses were well bunched. But, as they came nearer, a sorrel and a bay pulled out in front, with the same gray gelding Figure had nosed out in the walking race close behind and coming on. Where the roadway widened out in front of the schoolhouse, the gray swung wide and came on in a driving finish.

FIGURE | 57

He crossed the line a full length in the lead, leaving tracks that showed a fourteen-foot stride.

Bob Evans had no doubts about winning the second heat, but the runoff match against the gray gelding worried him as he jogged the little stallion out to the starting line. Figure could never match that fourteen-foot stride, and the gelding had been gaining speed when he crossed the finish line. The only chance for a short-legged horse would be in getting a quick start, gaining a long lead, then having the courage to stave off the gray's powerful, driving finish. Beyond his size and stride, the gelding would have a tremendous advantage. He was a trained racer, and Figure was a novice. The gray would be carrying less than half as much weight, and he would have a good rest before the match; Figure would have little or none.

Figure had no more trouble in winning over the horses chosen for the second heat than Bob had expected. But what surprised him was the little horse's way of going. He showed no inclination to break into a gallop, needed no urging and, for a short-legged horse, the length of his stride was amazing. With each thrust of his powerful hind legs he drove his body upward as well as forward, so that all four feet were off the ground nearly half the time. His start from the line was not too good, but within a dozen lengths he had pulled out in front of the pack, taken the middle of the roadway, and was increasing his lead with every stride. At the halfway mark he was five lengths out in front, then Bob slacked him off a bit to save his strength for the match with the gray.

There are few sports more exciting than a race between two evenly matched horses, and though Figure was given little chance against the gelding, the crowd watched eagerly as the stubby-legged bay and the tall gray jogged out to the starting line for the runoff.

The experience Bob Evans had gained in the first run helped him in planning the second. With only two horses in the race there would be no fight for position, but the race might easily be lost right at the start. The gray would gain speed slowly, for his long legs and flat muscles would not give him quick leverage, but once his full speed had been reached no short, bunchy-muscled horse could stay with him. If Figure were to win he must do it in

FIGURE | 59

the first half of the race, and to do that he must be gotten away from the line in a lightning-fast start. The question was how to make him do it. If he were hit, he would doubtlessly start off at a gallop and be disqualified; if he started off as he had in the first race, he would surely be beaten. They had almost reached the big pine when reason came to Bob's rescue: a horse was a creature of habits; he would do what he had been trained to do, and Figure had been trained to pull stumps.

At the starting line the gray danced and bobbed his head nervously. Figure stood quietly, feet planted solidly, head high, muscles drawn tense, and one ear turned back for Bob's command.. It came sharply at the instant the starter flung down his hat: "Hup boy! Hit it!"

With the same explosive power he used for yanking a stump loose, Figure sprang away from the line. Before the gray could collect himself for a start the little stallion's sharp hoofs were clicking like castanets and throwing back chips of frozen dirt.

At the halfway mark Figure was a good four lengths in front, but the tide of the race was turning. The gelding had reached full stride and was coming on in a storm of speed. Bob slackened the reins a trifle, pressed his knees tighter, and moved his weight forward. Figure's ears came back flat to his neck, the tempo of his hoofbeats quickened, and Bob could feel his stride lengthen — but still the gray gelding came on. At the schoolhouse the gap had been shortened to a single length, and where the roadway widened the gray swung out to make his passing bid. The sound of hoofbeats was lost in the shouting of the crowd as the gray's head inched forward along Figure's rump and past his hip. In desperation Bob leaned forward along the little bay's neck, and with his mouth close to the pinned-back ears he barked, "Hup boy! Hit it! Hit it!"

And Figure hit it. Muzzle stretched forward, legs driving and nostrils flaring, he staved off the gelding's final rush by no more than a handbreadth until the finish line was safely crossed.

Except for those who were saddling their horses for the running race, the pioneers crowded around the little bay stallion that wouldn't be beaten. Women and children patted his heaving sides, while the men thumped Bob Evans on the back and congratulated him on the fine ride he had made. But

FIGURE | 61

Bob Evans had no time for congratulations. "Leave me out o' here!" he shouted. "I got to git back there for the next race, and I don't aim to run him on the way out."

"Don't be a fool, Bob!" someone shouted. "After what he's a'ready done you'd kill him, and he ain't got a chance ag'in them race hosses. The best in the Green Mountains is here!"

"Leave me out o' here!" Bob shouted again. "There ain't nothin' short of a bullet could kill this little hoss — nor stop him from winnin' neither. I'm betting one to ten he can outrun ary hoss in the White River Valley."

With everything he owned in the world bet on the race, Bob jogged Figure out to the starting line again. A dozen high-spirited race horses danced and reared as their light riders tried to line them up for the start. Among them Figure looked like a pony that had slipped into the excited crowd by mistake. He stood quietly while Bob dismounted to cut a switch, and he showed no sign of nervousness when he was ridden to his place near the center of the line. As the starter counted off "One! Two! Three!" Bob raised his switch, and Figure set his muscles for the start. At the shout of *Go!* Bob cut the switch down across Figure's rump, and he leaped away from the line like an arrow from a bowstring.

Figure had never before been hit with a whip, and there was no reason for Bob to hit him again. For a quick start his short, heavily muscled legs gave him a tremendous advantage over the taller, less rugged race horses. Within half a dozen leaps he had pulled a length in front of the pack, gained the center of the roadway, and was increasing his lead a few inches at every leap. Bob lay low above Figure's neck, keeping his weight over the withers, and urging him on with his voice. But Figure needed no urging. Before the other horses in the race could get into full stride he had opened a gap of four lengths between himself and the pack. At the halfway mark he had stretched it to five lengths. And he was still five lengths in front when he streaked past the wildly shouting crowd in front of the tavern.

No one knew or cared which horse finished second. As the crowd gathered around for a better look at the little horse that could outpull, outwalk,

FIGURE | 63

outtrot, and outrun any other horse in the Green
Mountains, a few men slipped away to Justin
Morgan's tavern. The previous fall no one of them
would have given five dollars for the chunky bay
colt with stubby legs. Now each man was anxious
to be first to make his offer — and for many times
five dollars. But Justin Morgan was an honest man.
He'd made a deal to rent Figure to Bob Evans for
two years, and he wouldn't go back on his deal.

After winning every event at the Randolph fair,
Figure's reputation spread like gossip through the
Vermont frontier. But he was seldom called Figure.

Some people called him Justin Morgan's horse, but he was usually referred to as the Morgan horse. The following spring the fastest horses to be found in the new state of Vermont were brought to race against "the Morgan horse." Whether at the walk, trot, or gallop, he beat every one of them. And his fame spread throughout the other New England states.

There were then no race tracks such as we have now, but a great many more horse races. The early American settlers took great pride in the speed of their driving horses, and it was considered a disgrace to be passed on the road. All that was necessary to start a race was for two men with fast horses to meet on a straight stretch of road. Often these races were run on the main streets of the towns or villages. Excitement ran high, and the betting often ran higher. When a man's horse became champion in his own neighborhood, he would often drive a hundred miles or more to match it in a race against some other famous champion.

By 1796 the reputation of "the Morgan horse" had spread as far as New York State. When it was discovered that Figure was to run in the races at the Brookfield, Vermont, fair, two of the fastest

FIGURE | 65

horses in New York were taken there to be matched against him. One of them was Sweepstakes, from Long Island; the other was Jonas Seely's famous brown filly, Silvertail, from Orange County, New York.

In the first match Figure outran Sweepstakes easily, and if there was any bet made between the owners of the two horses, there is no record of it. But Jonas Seely refused to race Silvertail unless Justin Morgan would bet fifty dollars on Figure. The bet was made, and again Figure won easily, but Seely claimed that Silvertail didn't have a fair start. Mr. Morgan then offered to bet him fifty dollars each on three more races: one at the gallop, one at the trot, and one at the walk. But Jonas Seely had had enough. He harnessed his flashy brown filly and drove her back to Orange County, where there was no stubby-legged little Morgan horse named Figure.

4

The Doctors' Horse

FOR TWO YEARS Bob Evans worked Figure in the woods nearly every day, taking out only time enough to visit local fairs and enter him in pulling and racing competitions. Then Justin Morgan died, leaving debts which his widow could not pay. Figure was taken in settlement of a debt and moved to Woodstock. There he worked in the woods and on farms for five years, competed at nearby fairs, and sired numerous colts at a fee of a dollar or two.

Very often there is only one man who can bring out the best efforts of a horse — and sometimes the situation is reversed. Figure brought out the best efforts of Bob Evans. Bob not only grieved when the little bay stallion was taken away from Randolph but resolved to save money until, someday, he could buy and own him. It took him five years to do it.

Then during the year that followed the two old friends worked their hearts out, clearing a worthless farm that Bob had rented, plowing it, cultivating, and trying to coax a crop from the rocky land. But it was a losing battle. By the end of the year Bob was again in debt, was sued by his creditors, and Figure was taken away from him.

Figure's fortunes suffered with those of Bob Evans. At the time Bob lost him he was eleven years old, well beyond the age when most horses have passed their prime. But Figure's longest and hardest years were still ahead of him. During the remainder of his life he was sold or traded seven times, and was used almost continuously at the hardest work a horse of any age could be put to, that of hauling freight over the rugged mountain roads as part of a six-horse team.

Most horses broke down after a year or two of freight hauling. Figure not only stood up to the grueling work for seventeen years but during that time sired an untold number of colts. When he reached the age of twenty-eight he was as sound as the granite beneath the mountains of his homeland, and as vigorous as a three-year-old. That winter was severely cold, and when not on the road he and his teammates were kept in an open corral. One night another horse kicked him in the flank, injuring him internally. With care and stabling, his life might have been saved, but his owner left him untended in the corral, and he died of his injury.

As with Lincoln and Shakespeare, a man's outstanding greatness often goes unrecognized during his lifetime. The same is true of horses. Figure stands alone in history as the only individual ever to have sired an entire breed of unique and superior horses. Beyond that, all three of the other distinct and superior horse breeds which have originated in this country are, at least in part, his descendants. Yet, during his lifetime he was never considered to be anything more than an oddly shaped, strutting little horse who could outpull any other horse of his size, and could outwalk, outtrot, and outrun any horse ever matched against him. No one — unless it was Bob Evans — realized that he looked odd only because he was unlike other horses in appearance and action, or that he embodied an entirely new type of compactness and beauty.

It was not until nearly twenty years after Figure's

death that his true greatness began to be appreciated. By that time his descendants, thousands of them, were the most highly prized horses in New England, for they had inherited his marvelous strength and speed, together with his high foot action, proud head carriage, beauty, gentle disposition, and courage.

Up to that time no one had questioned his ancestry, or cared a penny's worth what it might have been. But as soon as his greatness became apparent horsemen renamed him Justin Morgan, in honor of the man who brought him to Vermont, and began trying to piece together a pedigree for him. Most of the information they gathered was from hearsay and the conflicting testimony of old men who thought they remembered him as a yearling colt. For more than a century a battle has raged as to whether his sire was a Thoroughbred, a Dutch horse, or just a mongrel. But the battle is all in vain, for a mutant neither inherits nor passes on to his offspring the same characteristics as those of his ancestors.

Although Figure's feats of strength and speed outstripped those of any other American horse of his time, his greatness arose from his prepotency — the ability of one parent to dominate in passing on characteristics to offspring. He not only possessed prepotency to an amazing degree but so strongly endowed his offspring with it that, sixty years after his death, James Ladd, a famous Kentucky horseman, wrote: "I see horses every day with perhaps a thirty-second part of the blood of Justin Morgan, but there it is, still predominating; there is the Morgan still so plainly seen that he who runs may read. Every close observer, every discerning judge of horses I meet, be he an admirer or a despiser of the Morgan, always admits this wonderful tendency in his blood."

There is no way of estimating how many colts Justin Morgan sired during the twenty-eight years of his life, but there must have been nearly a thousand of them. Some of the mares who bore these colts were of excellent quality for their time. Others were common farm horses, some fairly large and some small, but regardless of what the mother might have been the colts were predominantly Morgan. And in turn their offspring was dominated by Morgan characteristics.

It is probable that most of Justin Morgan's colts spent their lives as he spent his: pulling stumps, hauling heavy loads over rough roads, or serving as some frontiersman's driving horse. Even so, numerous of his sons were of such outstanding quality that they were kept as sires. The three most famous of these sires were Sherman Morgan, Bullrush Morgan, and Woodbury Morgan. Each of them headed a distinct branch of the Morgan family that was noted for its beauty, speed, gentleness, strength, endurance, and courage. But in each family one or two of these characteristics of Justin Morgan stood out more sharply than in the others.

Sherman Morgan became the most famous of the

three, for in addition to the other Morgan qualities, the family that he headed had a wide streak of "ham" in it. No actor ever loved the applause of an audience more than it has been loved by the descendants of this proud little horse. His blood is largely accountable for the pride, boldness, and showiness of the five-gaited saddle horses that we now see "strutting their stuff" in our finest horse shows. From their earliest beginnings it was necessary only to put Sherman Morgan's descendants in harness, under saddle, or in the show ring to have them become the peacocks of the horse world, and their speed at the trot was dazzling.

Sherman Morgan's son, Black Hawk, was the finest show horse and the fastest trotter in New England. And Black Hawk's son, Ethan Allen, became the world's champion trotting stallion. He was a compact, short-legged little horse, but made up for lack of size in courage and style of traveling at the trot. The attention of the entire nation was called to the Morgan breed when, in 1859, Ethan Allen defeated the world's champion trotting mare, Flora Temple, and put an end to her career. Morgan horses immediately came into the greatest demand of any breed in America. Hundreds upon hundreds of them were used as cavalry mounts in the Civil War, and more than a few were chosen by generals in both the North and South as their war chargers.

Well before the Civil War the frontiers of America had been pushed westward beyond the Missouri River. Towns and villages dotted the countryside, great cities had sprung up, and railroads were being built, but the horse still furnished ninety per cent of the transportation.

As the population grew, the demand for faster and better transportation grew apace. The railroads were unable to meet the demand, but the Morgan horse stepped forward to fill the breach for the next half century. In the North, where roadways threaded from village to village, Justin Morgan's descendants became the most popular of all fine harness horses, but there were far too few Morgans to supply the demand. To bridge the gap, horsemen began mating Morgan sires with good light-harness mares from stock that had already been improved by an infusion of Thoroughbred blood. These matings resulted in a new and distinct type of horse: the almost perfect road horse of the 1880's and '90's.

These roadsters inherited the longer legs and more refined bodies of the Thoroughbred, but retained the gentle disposition, the beauty, stylish action, animation, hardiness, and tireless endurance of the Morgan. From both Thoroughbred and Morgan they inherited courage, remarkable speed, and determination to keep going until the last ounce of strength was spent.

At that time American men took the same pride in the speed and beauty of their horses that they now take in fine automobiles. Every man who could afford them had a matched pair of swift and beauti-

ful roadsters in his stable, together with a brightly polished top-buggy, cariole, or phaeton. He took his greatest pride in driving his family to church, or in taking his friends for a long Sunday afternoon's ride through the woods and farm lands, behind a high-stepping pair of flashy trotters.

In every great city there was one particular street where the young blades raced their sleek roadsters in "brushes" with each other, just as they now gun their hot-rods in drag races. On warm summer evenings New York's Central Park echoed to the fast beat of trotting hoofs, and on their high seats silk-hatted coachmen held the reins above a span of spanking roadsters, as the wealthy smiled and nodded to one another from gleaming phaetons.

To many of these people the fast and flashy roadster was a luxury: a man's means of displaying his success in life — or that of his father. But to one man the fast and tireless roadster was an absolute necessity. That man was the country doctor. Most of his patients were farmers or woodsmen, and country roads were seldom more than a pair of rough wheel tracks, winding through swamps, meadows, and woodlands. In spring these roads were often ankle deep in mud. In winter they were drifted high with snow. But regardless of the weather, these country doctors made the round of their patients day after day, though they often had to drive fifty or sixty miles to do it. And often the life of a patient depended upon the speed with which a doctor's horse could get him to some backwoods cabin.

The fine-quality roadster made the ideal doctors' horse. The high action of his gait, his strength, his courage, and his almost unbelievable endurance made it possible for him to travel long distances over rough roads at a speed no other horse except a true Morgan was ever able to match. It is not surprising that this type of horse soon came to be known as the Doctors' Horse.

In New England a story has long been told of a country doctor who owned a remarkable pair of roadsters. No doubt they were largely of Morgan blood, for he had named them Sherman and Ethan.

The winter of 1895 was severe in New England. Before Christmas the ponds and rivers froze to a depth of more than three feet, but there was very little snow. Then, soon after New Year's, one blizzard followed another, until the snow drifted ten or twelve feet deep in many places. The blizzards had no sooner stopped than the weather turned bitterly cold, with temperatures ranging from twenty to thirty degrees below zero.

When the weather was at its coldest, a tree fell on a French-Canadian woodchopper, far in the backwoods of Maine, breaking and badly crushing one of his legs. His partner carried him to their shanty, then left him alone while he snowshoed fifteen miles to town for the doctor. It was midnight before he reached the doctor's house, completely exhausted, and with both feet badly frozen.

The doctor had the half-frozen woodchopper put to bed and gave him a strong stimulant. Then as he treated his feet he questioned him about his injured partner. The questioning was almost as difficult a task as saving the feet, for the man spoke no English, and the doctor no French-Canadian.

When, at last, the doctor discovered the extent of the injury and that the man had been left alone in a backwoods shack, he knew that he must reach him with the least possible delay if his life were to be saved. A crushed leg was one of the most dangerous injuries a woodsman could suffer, for the flow of blood through the limb was usually stopped. Even though the patient were given the best of care, gangrene would set in unless the circulation could be restored quickly. And if gangrene developed, the leg must be amputated under absolutely sanitary conditions.

All through the night the doctor treated his patient, drawing the frost slowly from his feet, massaging them, and stimulating the flow of blood necessary to save them. And as he worked he drew from the man, as best he could, directions for finding the way to his shanty. At daybreak he had Sherman and

Ethan hitched to a stout sleigh, bundled himself in a heavy fur coat, and set out for the shanty in the backwoods. No one had traveled the roads since the blizzards. Their course could be determined only by an occasional fence post, tall enough to stick up through the snow, or where the roadway had been cut through woodlands.

Hour after hour the horses plunged and floundered through snow that was belly deep. Often the doctor lost the road entirely, or was forced to turn far away from it in order to get around impassable snowdrifts. He lost nearly an hour in finding a place where the horses could cross a deeply-gouged and icebound brook. It was late in the afternoon when, with no stop for feeding and only an occasional halt to catch their wind, Ethan and Sherman fought their way to the woodchoppers' shanty. No other type of horse, except the hardiest mustangs or pure-blooded Morgans, could have made it through at all.

When the doctor reached the shanty he found the woodchopper in a bunk half filled with dirty straw, unconscious and nearly frozen to death. The only way of heating the shack was a little sheet-iron stove on which the men had done their cooking —

and, as might have been expected, there was no firewood cut. There was no water except what could be melted from snow, no bedding except a few ragged deerskins, and the woodchopper's leg was already swollen to double its normal size.

Gangrene had set in, but amputation was impossible under such filthy conditions. There was only one course open to the doctor: the man must be revived, his leg splinted, and an effort made to stimulate any possible circulation. Then, if the patient's life were to be saved, he must be taken out of the woods without a moment's delay. The doctor realized that the trip would take most of the night, but with a trail now broken he believed the horses would be able to make it. If not, they could probably reach some farmhouse where there would be heat, water, and clean bedclothing.

The doctor wrapped the injured man in his own fur coat, laid him out as comfortably as possible on the floor of the sleigh, and started the return trip just as night fell. The going for the horses was easier than on the way out, but they still had to flounder belly deep wherever the snow was drifted, and they could cover no more than two miles an hour. Before the first hour had passed, darkness settled down, so black that the doctor couldn't see the horses' heads. He could only trust to their intelligence, letting them find their way the best they could, while he tried to keep the injured man conscious and alive.

It seemed to the doctor that a couple of hours had passed, and he was kneeling to care for his patient when the sleigh suddenly pitched downward. The next instant there was the sound of thrashing in the darkness, a shrill squeal of pain, and the sleigh nearly tipped over as it came to a teetering stop. The doctor didn't need to see in order to know what had happened. One of the horses had slipped and fallen when going down into the icebound brook gorge, and the squeal could mean one thing only: he had broken a leg.

Sherman was down, pounding his head into the snow in his pain, and one hind leg lay crumpled under him. The doctor didn't let him suffer long. Within a minute he had filled a syringe and plunged the needle deep behind an ear, where its point would be sure to reach the brain.

At first the situation seemed hopeless. If they

should stay where they were, the injured man would certainly die before morning, and the doctor himself would probably freeze to death. Of course, he could have mounted Ethan and saved himself, but the thought never entered his mind; the welfare of his patient stood above everything else. He believed that, with shafts fitted to the sleigh, a single horse — if he were a strong one, well fed and rested — might possibly be able to pull it over the partly broken trail. Without shafts, however, and for a horse that had fought snowdrifts for twelve hours without food or rest, the task seemed impossible.

Impossible or not, it had to be tried, in hope that

a farmhouse might be reached before the wood-chopper died. The doctor broke the pole of the sleigh short, fastened Ethan's singletree to the stub, and picked up the reins. At his cluck the good horse dug his hoofs in, bowed his neck, and dragged the sleigh over his dead mate's body, across the frozen brook, and up the steep bank on the far side.

In the blackness the doctor had no way of knowing where they might be, or whether Ethan was following the trail made on the way out. His only hope of finding a farmhouse was by sighting the light from some nearby window. But New England farmers go early to bed in winter, and no light was sighted.

On and on Ethan plunged and floundered, dragging the careening sleigh behind him. Now and again he stopped for a few moments, caught his breath, and then plunged on again. And hour after hour the half-frozen doctor knelt beside his patient, stimulating him and keeping the spark of life from flickering out. The first gray of morning was lighting the sky when Ethan dragged the sleigh into the doctor's dooryard — and fell, completely exhausted, at the stable door.

5

The Trotters

STRANGELY ENOUGH, the churches were largely responsible for the creation of the first new horse breed to be developed in America. As early as 1750 English Thoroughbreds were being imported to Virginia and other southern colonies. Following the Revolutionary War, race tracks were laid out near the larger cities and Thoroughbred horse racing, with betting on the results, became the most popular sport in the South.

Southern ministers had no objection to these races, but in the North it was quite a different matter. Because of the betting, ministers of nearly every denomination preached against horse racing as a sin. They were successful in having anti-horse-race laws passed in several states, but they could do little about their own parishioners who had fast driving horses. Whenever two men with fast-steppers met on a roadway there was bound to be a race, and the parsons were obliged to look the other way. In time, trotting races came to be looked upon as an innocent entertainment, but galloping races were still considered sinful.

One man was refused membership in a church because he owned Thoroughbred race horses. When he pointed out to the minister that a man who was already a member of that church also had race horses, the parson answered, "Oh, yes, but his horses are trotting horses; yours are race horses."

With this look-the-other-way sanction of the churches, trotting races became the chief attraction of every county fair in the North. There were then no tracks at the fairs. The races were run on a nearby stretch of level road, the speed was never clocked, and no attention was paid to the type or breed of horse. Any man with a fast trotter could enter him, and betting — when the parson's back was turned — ran high. In an effort to win, horsemen who owned fast trotting mares began hunting out sires capable of increasing the speed of their colts. In this way the foundation for a new breed of horses was laid — now known as the Standard-bred. For more than eighty years the descendants of two great sires, Messenger and Justin Morgan, struggled for dominance of this new breed.

Messenger was a gray Thoroughbred, imported from England in 1788. He was a galloping race horse, not a trotter, and had never been outstanding for speed on the English tracks. He was a rather coarse, heavy-boned horse, with a stubby neck and a head that seemed too big for his body. Besides, he had a vicious temper, and is said to have killed a groom. At the time Justin Morgan was foaled, Messenger was stabled on Long Island, New York, and being mated with the local mares there, largely Dutch and Norfolk Trotter, but it was soon dis-covered that many of his offspring had remarkable speed at the trotting gait.

The struggle between the two great sires began in 1796, when Justin Morgan beat Silvertail, a grand-daughter of Messenger, at the Brookfield, Vermont, fair. No one watching that race had any idea that he was seeing the first battle in a war that would last nearly a century — one in which both sides would have to join forces before the final victory could be won.

In an effort to gain the greatest possible trotting speed, the fastest horses of every breed and type were crossed, but for nearly a half century the winners were horses that had not been bred for trotting speed. In New England they were Morgans, their mothers usually common farm mares. In New York they were largely descendants of Messenger, though their mothers were of various breeds and types.

The first trotting race on any track in the United States was a free-for-all held at the Union Course on Long Island in 1823. The distance was two miles, the prize one thousand dollars, and the horse who won it was the most unlikely imaginable.

Topgallant, a grandson of Messenger, had been a fairly good long-distance racer in his youth, but when he became aged he was sold to a Philadelphia hack driver. For several years he plodded up and down the city streets, with a younger and more spirited animal for his teammate. Toppy was fifteen years old when, one spring evening, the driver left his hack outside a tavern. While he was gone something startled the old horse's spirited mate, and he ran away. Always willing to oblige, Toppy went along, but he wasn't running away so there was no reason for him to be excited. As his mate raced down the cobbled street, scattering staid Philadelphians in all directions, old Toppy trotted along at his side, never once breaking into a gallop.

Horsemen were amazed that any horse, particularly a Thoroughbred racer, would hold a trotting gait while his mate ran at a fast gallop. They were even more surprised that any horse of Toppy's age could trot fast enough to keep up with a frightened galloper. It was this performance that led Topgallant's owner to enter him in the free-for-all trotting race at the Union Course. Once on the track, the old fellow forgot his age and pranced to the starting line as if he were a colt. He streaked across the finish line in the same way, becoming the first horse in the United States to win a trotting race on a race track. That was enough to retire him forever as a hack horse; he spent the rest of his life traveling around Pennsylvania, Virginia, and Maryland as a trotting race horse. There he won fame by trotting the first recorded three-minute mile.

The second of the strange horses to win fame as an American trotter was Dutchman. He was a descendant of Messenger, raised in New Jersey, but from his name and description it is probable that his mother was a Dutch work mare. When Dutchman was three years old he was sold to a Philadelphia building contractor. He spent several years hauling heavy loads of lumber and brick, but he didn't work well with a teammate. His mouth was like cast iron, and he was as headstrong as a mule.

Because of his bad manners Dutchman was taken out of the team and worked alone on a single wagon. This was much more to his liking, but it didn't help his driver much. If the old horse were headed toward his stable, he grabbed the bit in his teeth, stuck his nose out like a battering ram, and took off at a pounding trot. With his wagon bouncing wildly, and pedestrians scattering like frightened quail, Dutchman would go tearing down the middle of the street as fast as he could swing his awkward legs. His driver could no more stop him than he could have stopped a hurricane. Often some young blade with a fast-stepping trotter and a gleaming buggy swung alongside to give the old work horse a race, but there was no trotter in Philadelphia that could ever keep up with him. His owner finally decided to enter him in trotting races.

What Dutchman lacked in beauty and good manners he made up in determination, speed at the trot, and endurance. He reached the peak of his career in 1839, by which time trotting horses were often being raced in harness, sometimes hitched to high-wheeled carts, but more often to racing wagons. Dutchman

won his fame by trotting a mile in two minutes and twenty-eight seconds, making him the first horse in the world to break the two-and-a-half-minute barrier.

English horsemen believed reports of the fast time being made by Dutchman to be truthless American bragging. When a Philadelphia man wrote John Lawrence, a noted British racing authority, that an American horse had trotted a mile in two and a half minutes, Lawrence wrote back: "American miles must be shorter than English miles — no horse ever did, or ever will for that matter, trot an English mile in so short a space of time, else the excessive rapidity and friction of his feet would strike fire and set him ablaze."

English horsemen had much to learn about trotting speed, and American horses set about to teach them. The greatest spur to increased trotting speed in this country was rivalry between the Morgans and the Messengers. This rivalry was heightened when, in 1833, a colt which would become famous was born into each family. They were Black Hawk, the most famous grandson of Justin Morgan, and

Lady Suffolk, the speediest great-granddaughter of Messenger.

Black Hawk's greatness was evident from the day he was foaled. By the time he was three he was not only the most beautiful show horse ever to have been seen in New England, but the fastest trotter. After he had beaten the best in New England he was taken to the New York State Fair and matched in a three-heat race against the Morse Horse, one of Messenger's fastest great-grandsons. Excitement ran high, for it was generally believed that the race would determine the supremacy between the Morgans and Messengers. The Morse Horse won the first heat, but Black Hawk easily ran away from him in the second and third. The remainder of Black Hawk's races were at New England fairs, and there is no record of his fastest time, but he was the first stallion to sire three colts who broke the two-and-a-half-minute trotting barrier.

While Black Hawk was becoming famous in New England, Lady Suffolk was pulling a butcher's cart in Smithtown on Long Island. She was later sold to a livery stable owner, and her speed was not discovered until she was hired by a New York newspaper owner who was in a hurry to get out to the race track. She, like Messenger, was gray, but she inherited none of his vicious disposition or coarseness. She was a refined lady in every respect — beautifully mannered, intelligent, fine-boned, and slender, but with powerful driving muscles in her back and quarters.

Lady Suffolk might well be called the pioneer of American harness racers, for she not only established the ideal conformation but set the speed mark from which the new breed took its name. Because she repeatedly trotted a mile in two minutes and a half, that speed was fixed as standard by the horsemen who wrote the bylaws and set up a registry for the breed. A horse, though of any type or ancestry, could be registered as a Standardbred if, and only if, it could trot or pace a mile in two and a half minutes.

Beyond this, "the Lady" was responsible for the discontinuance of trotting races under saddle. Because of her delicate build she could attain greater speed when drawing a light cart than when being ridden. For this reason some of the country's finest wainwrights began making very light, high-wheeled racing carts. These marked a big step forward in the speed of trotting races.

Lady Suffolk, because of her repeated breaking of the time barrier, was generally recognized as the world's champion trotting horse. With her rise to fame the New York horsemen were loud in their claim that Messenger had been proved the greatest sire of trotting speed ever known. The New Englanders pointed to Black Hawk's defeat of the Morse Horse, and were as loud in their claim that the honor belonged to Justin Morgan.

When the shouting was at its loudest a little mongrel mare named Flora Temple popped up to take the glory away from both great sires. She was bobtailed, and so unmanageable that she was sold as a four-year-old for thirteen dollars. But when put with a good trainer she dominated the harness-racing tracks of America for ten years, repeatedly broke her own world's records, and cut Lady Suffolk's best time by a full ten seconds. During the height of her reign the New England horsemen did little bragging about the speed of their Morgans. But the New Yorkers were louder than ever in their claims of victory, for Flora Temple, although there was no drop of Messenger blood in her veins, had been born in Orange County, New York. The New Englanders had to keep quiet until 1861; then it became their turn to shout.

In 1849 Black Hawk had sired Ethan Allen, who is said to have been almost a duplicate of Justin Morgan in size and appearance. For a short-legged horse he had incredible speed at the trot, together with high, flashy foot action, boundless courage, and brilliant showmanship. For several years he and his father competed for top honors at the New England fairs. Then when Black Hawk became too old to compete, Ethan Allen reigned supreme. No horse in New England could match his style and beauty in the show ring, and none could approach his speed at the trot. Because there seldom were tracks at these fairs, his speed was exhibited almost entirely on country roads. In these exhibitions he was hitched to a light wagon and paired with a galloping polemate named Socks. Ethan's proud carriage and high foot action made him a beautiful performer, and it was a stirring sight to watch him trotting abreast of a mate that was racing all-out at the gallop.

Year by year, all through the 1850's, Ethan Allen increased his trotting speed, and Flora Temple broke her own speed records almost as rapidly as she set them. With each brilliant performance by Ethan Allen the New Englanders raised a shout of victory. They claimed that Flora Temple's time was best only because she was raced on perfectly conditioned tracks, while Ethan's performances were on rough country roads. The New Yorkers pooh-poohed the idea, claiming that having a running mate to pull the wagon more than made up for the advantage of a race track.

In 1861 the argument was brought to a showdown. Flora Temple and Ethan Allen were at last matched against each other in a race of three one-mile heats — she hitched to the lightest possible sulky, he and his running mate to a light wagon. Ethan won, but in doing it Flora forced him to match the fastest mile she had ever trotted — less than two minutes and twenty seconds.

The New Englanders went wild with Ethan

Allen's victory over Flora Temple, but their joy was short-lived. New York produced another world's trotting champion, Dexter, to break Flora Temple's record by more than two seconds. To delight the New Yorkers even more, Dexter was a descendant of Messenger. Again the war for trotting supremacy between the Morgans and the Messengers flared to white heat.

Ethan Allen was the only hope of the Morgan backers, but Ethan by that time was sixteen years old. Even so, his backers clamored until a match was arranged between him and Dexter, under the

same conditions as against Flora Temple. Again
Ethan won, clipping his time for the fastest heat to
two minutes and fifteen seconds — the fastest mile
ever to have been trotted by any horse.

There was nothing for the New Yorkers to do but
to go home, lick their wounds, and hunt for a horse
that might be able to outtrot the seemingly ageless
Ethan Allen. Strangely enough the horse they chose
was a descendant of Silvertail, Jonas Seely's mare
whom Justin Morgan had soundly beaten at the
Brookfield, Vermont, fair in 1796.

Soon after Silvertail was beaten by Justin Morgan,

Jonas Seely mated her with Bishop's Hambletonian, one of Messenger's finest sons. From this mating she produced a nervous, high-strung filly, who in her unruliness injured an eye and was named One Eye. One Eye also produced a fast, high-strung filly — later named the Kent Mare — who was so unmanageable that she lamed herself permanently in a runaway.

Since the Kent Mare was worthless for work or driving, Jonas Seely decided to try producing a colt from her, but he had little confidence in the result, so mated her to the cheapest sire nearby. This sire was Abdallah, a vicious, ungainly stallion, later sold to a fish peddler for five dollars.

It has long been known that inbreeding will often concentrate all the best or all the worst characteristics in a horse family. Abdallah was an outstanding example. His mother was Messenger's most famous granddaughter, and his father was Messenger's most famous son, but every bad quality of the old English Thoroughbred was concentrated in this one offspring. It is not surprising that Jonas Seely expected a poor colt from the mating, for the Kent Mare was not only unmanageable and a cripple, but she too was an inbred descendant of Messenger — so her colt would be doubly inbred.

At the time the Kent Mare's colt was born Mr. Seely had a hired man named Bill Rysdyk. Bill wasn't very bright, couldn't read or write, and didn't have a penny, but he wanted to own horses of his own. Jonas Seely, being a rather sharp trader, made a deal with him. He sold Bill Rysdyk the mare and colt for $125, taking in payment a long-term note. Bill was the proudest man in the world, and named the colt Hambletonian.

As soon as Bill had worked out his debt, he quit his job and went into the horse business — with one crippled mare and her awkward, long-legged yearling colt who stood two inches higher at the hips than at the withers. It was not long, however, until Bill Rysdyk had reason to be proud: his colt won a five-dollar prize as the best two-year-old stallion at the Orange County, New York, fair. Still better, the colt showed surprising speed at the trot, and he had inherited none of the bad disposition of his parents.

The next year Rysdyk's colt won again, but a newspaper reporter was not much impressed by him. He wrote: "Hamiltonian has a handsome movement and fine color and is of much better form than most of the stallions exhibited, but he lacks — and this is a family failing — that muscular swelling of the thighs and steam-engine motion of the hocks which propel horses along over a distance of ground."

The reporter was probably familiar with the chunkiness and steam-engine action of the Morgans, and could not appreciate value in the long, flat muscles this almost purebred colt had inherited from his Thoroughbred ancestors. Hambletonian made Bill Rysdyk a rich man, and proved the value of those flat muscles by founding the Hambletonian strain of harness racers, the most famous trotting and pacing horses in the world.

When Hambletonian was six years old he was mated with Dolly Spanker, a fast-stepping roadster whose owner used her as a driving mare. The colt of this mating was named Robert Fillingham (later changed to George Wilkes). He, like his father, stood higher at the hips than at the withers. He was also long-legged and long-backed, but more solidly built, stouter in the loin, stepped with a higher action of his feet, and lacked the high-strung nervousness that marked many of Hambletonian's offspring.

Actually, Robert Fillingham verged on laziness, and showed no indication of greatness until he was put into the hands of Horace Jones for training. At first Horace had little success with the colt. If he took a notion to do his best he could trot to beat the band, but he seldom took the notion, and no amount of coaxing or whipping would put it into his head. In training he would often trot the first three quarters of a mile in excellent time, but could never be induced to make a winning sprint in the home stretch.

Many horsemen believe that more than half the credit for every winning race belongs to the horse's trainer, and to its rider or driver. A horse may have inherited the bone, muscle, and courage that make him an almost perfect racing machine, but he cannot inherit the intelligence either to develop his natural speed to its fullest extent or to control it.

Horace Jones was a great trainer, and it didn't take him long to discover the key that would unlock Robert Fillingham's speed. The colt had a

phobia: he was frightened by the shadow of another horse coming up on him from behind — and
when frightened he could really burn up the track.
Opposite the three-quarter pole of the Fashion
Course on Long Island there was a big tree, with
thick branches extending nearly to the ground. On
training days Jones had Rube, a fast-starting race
horse, mounted by a light rider and hidden behind
the big tree. The moment Horace had passed the
tree, the rider would whip Rube out onto the track
and close alongside Robert Fillingham. The instant
the colt caught sight of the shadow moving up
beside him he would become frightened and try to
run away from it. With Rube's shadow to spur him
into a sprint down the home stretch he turned in
some surprisingly fast miles, and New York horsemen believed he could outtrot even Ethan Allen.
They put up a big purse for a matched race between
the two horses, but insisted that it be trotted on the
Fashion Course, and that Ethan trot without his
mate.

The race between Ethan Allen and Robert Fillingham was run on September 10, 1862. No trotting
race on earth had ever before created so much at-

tention and excitement, for this was not merely a match between two fast trotting horses. It was for the trotting supremacy of the world between New York's Hambletonians — almost pure Thoroughbred — and New England's Morgans. It is estimated that more than $150,000 was wagered on the race; the grandstand was filled to overflowing, and thousands stood along the edge of the racing strip.

As "Black Dan" Mace drove Ethan Allen onto the track the New Englanders, and more than a few of the New Yorkers, went wild. The applause was all that was needed to bring out the ham in the proud little grandson of Sherman Morgan. Ethan Allen's head and tail went up, and he lifted each hoof with the grace of a concert conductor wielding a baton. In comparison, Robert Fillingham looked like a tired hack horse when Horace Jones drove him through the crowd and onto the track. He showed neither excitement nor interest in the cheering of the crowd, but plodded to the starting line as if he were pulling a milk cart down a village street.

At the starter's shout of *Go!* Ethan Allen flew away from the line with his short legs driving like pistons of a runaway steam engine. Behind him

Robert Fillingham seemed to be having trouble in getting his long legs untracked and moving in rhythm. At the quarter-mile post Ethan Allen was out in front by half a dozen lengths, and still widening the gap. At the half he was still six lengths ahead, but Robert Fillingham had found his rhythm, and his longer stride was beginning to tell. Going into the far turn he was whittling the gap down a bit, but the crowd could see that his heart wasn't in the race, that he wasn't putting out his best effort.

New Yorkers began reaching for their pocketbooks when Robert Fillingham trailed Ethan Allen by four lengths as they came around the near turn and into the home stretch. It was here that the big tree stood, behind which old Rube was hidden on training days. Robert Fillingham didn't wait for Rube's hated shadow to sneak up beside him. He had formed the habit of turning on the speed at the moment he passed that tree, and now he turned it on in earnest. His forehoofs reached out as if he were trying to escape a demon, and the drive of his powerful hind legs shot him forward more than twenty feet at every stride. Halfway down the home stretch he passed Ethan Allen like a jack rabbit pass-

ing a prairie dog, and crossed the finish line two lengths in front.

The second heat of the race was almost a duplicate of the first. The third heat was hardly a race at all; at the finish Horace Jones pulled Robert Fillingham down and won the race at a jogging gait. Ethan Allen had proved himself to be a great trotter, and amazingly fast in the early stages of a race, but with his short legs — and without his polemate to pull the racing wagon — he was unable to match the Hambletonian's speed in the final sprint.

It was believed at that time, and is still believed by many horsemen, that this race proved the descendants of Rysdyk's Hambletonian to have much greater speed at the trot than the descendants of Justin Morgan. What it actually proved was that a fusing of the blood of these two great sires would produce the fastest harness horses ever known — for Dolly Spanker, Robert Fillingham's mother, was a Morgan. Since that famous race there has never been a doubt that the male-line (sons of sons of sons) descendants of Rysdyk's Hambletonian have been the best harness-racing horses on earth —

but to produce the very fastest and finest there has always been a strong infusion of Morgan blood from the dam's side of the matings.

From generation to generation the speed of the Standardbreds has been increased until now the mark of greatness in harness racers, both trotters and pacers, is the ability to break the two-minute-mile barrier. It has been broken by about fifty trotters and ninety pacers. Every trotter on the list, and all but four or five of the pacers, carries the blood of Justin Morgan in his veins, and it is now almost impossible to find a topnotch harness racer that is not a male-line descendant of Messenger.

Greyhound, who has held the world's trotting championship since 1938, is descended in a straight male line from Rysdyk's Hambletonian, but in his ancestry he traces in a dozen lines on the dam's side to Justin Morgan. His record for the mile is one minute and fifty-five and one-fourth seconds, but, contrary to the Englishman's belief, the excessive rapidity and friction of his feet have never struck fire and set him ablaze.

6

The Horse Americans Made

SINCE LONG BEFORE recorded history men have selected and developed animals so as to best serve their needs. The early settlers in the northern colonies crossbred various types of horses brought here from Europe in order to develop a general-purpose animal — one that could work in the fields or woods and also pull a wagon rapidly over rough roads. In the South the need was exactly opposite. There the farming was done on great plantations, and the climate in the summer was so hot that mules, far tougher animals, were much more suitable than horses for heavy work. Then too, there were few roads, so most of the traveling was done on horseback.

What the plantation owners needed was a highly specialized saddle horse. It must be so gentle, sure-footed, and easy-gaited that a lady could ride it with absolute comfort and safety, yet strong enough to carry a heavy man all day as he rode from field to field in managing his workers. But there had never been such a horse. The desert breeds were too hot-blooded and nervous to be safe as a lady's mount. The gaits of a trotter were too jolting and tiring. A pacer was even less suitable. The low movement of its feet made it inclined to stumble on uneven ground, and though its slow amble was very comfortable to the rider, its fast gait was horribly uncomfortable.

A horse's gait is governed by a pattern that is in his brain at birth. If a colt's ancestors have been pacers, he will pace instinctively; if trotters, he will trot. But if he has both trotters and pacers in his ancestry he will be born with both patterns in his brain, though usually one will dominate. Such a colt may be an instinctive pacer, but he is apt to trot if obliged to hurry over uneven or muddy ground. Or, although an instinctive trotter, he will often pace when hurrying downhill. With this knowledge, Southern horsemen set out to develop a horse ideally suited to their needs.

To make their horses multiple-gaited they crossed the finest trotting horses to be found in Virginia, the Carolinas, and Georgia with the best Narragansett Pacers of Rhode Island. To gain grace of motion, high foot action, long stride, and the most elastic gait possible, they selected animals with long necks, high withers, flexible pasterns, and extremely sloping shoulders. To assure the strength necessary for carrying a heavy rider, they hunted out horses with short backs, stout loins, flat croups, and excellent legs. To provide endurance they demanded that a horse be deep in the girth and well-sprung in the ribs, allowing ample room for heart and lungs. And above all, they insisted upon horses with gentle dispositions.

When, through careful crossbreeding, a colt having all the desirable qualities was produced, the Southern horsemen taught him to perform gaits which were entirely unnatural to any horse. They were based upon a combination of the trotting and pacing gaits, and were so designed as to give the horse high foot action but eliminate every particle of jolt to the rider.

Teaching a horse the complicated patterns of a

man-made gait requires exceptional skill and end-
less patience, for the most intelligent horse can learn
only one new movement at a time. He can remember it only after it has been repeated so many times
that the pattern is marked deeply in his brain and
the movement can be performed without conscious
thought.

When a crossbred colt was old enough for training, he was harnessed with bridle, checkstraps, and
long reins, then driven in a paddock by his trainer.
Day after day the colt was schooled in short lessons
until he had learned to obey the slightest touch on
the reins, and to walk, trot, or back on command.
And each day the checkstraps were shortened a
trifle, drawing his head higher, tucking his chin
closer, and arching the crest of his neck.

When either man or animal holds his head
proudly erect, his whole body becomes animated;
his mind is alert and his muscles collected for instant
action; his back curves inward, his chest outward,
and he walks with a firmer, higher step. Much of
what horses lack in ability to remember they make
up for in their keen sense of association, and the
colt soon learned to associate the bit with the check-

straps. By the time his schooling with the long reins was completed, he needed no checkstraps; his head would come up and his whole body become animated the moment the bit was slipped into his mouth. He was then ready for a rider and his kindergarten lessons in gaiting.

We think of the walk as a natural gait — one at which a horse would need no training — but this is far from true of the proud, high-action walk of the five-gaited saddler. Often a colt was worked for months at the walk before being allowed to travel at any other gait. At first the lessons were very short, so the colt would not become tired or nervous, and he was never allowed to jig or dance, although the trainer urged him forward with his legs while holding him back lightly with the reins. The urging made him pick his feet up smartly, but the slight pressure on the reins slowed his forward motion, causing him to lift his hocks and knees higher, and to fold his feet back at the ankles. And each perfect step helped to mark the pattern more clearly in his brain.

During his training at the walk the colt learned to obey signals given him by various pressures and positions of his trainer's legs. With these aids it was not difficult to teach him to trot boldly and squarely. But weeks, and often months, of training were needed before the trot became a perfect two-beat rhythm — with every step a graceful, strutting pose — regardless of the speed at which the pupil was required to travel.

With the walk and trot nearly perfected, it was time for the colt to learn his first man-made gait, the rack. From his ancestors he had inherited the patterns for trotting and pacing, but this new gait would be a combination of both. Before learning to perform it he would need a bridle with a curb bit that would force him to carry his head higher than ever before, to tuck his chin closer, and to bend his neck in a swanlike curve. This would not only make him appear more graceful, but would shift more of his weight onto his hind legs, giving him the necessary balance for performing the new gait.

Of all the artificial gaits a horse may be taught, the most beautiful, the most comfortable to ride, and the most difficult to teach is the rack. To perform it, a horse must be taught to step forward as though he were going to pace, although moving his legs with a high action rather than a swinging motion. And instead of moving both lateral feet at the same moment, he must pause in his stride, so that his feet strike in an even four-beat rhythm. The action is difficult to explain in words; it is a thousand times more difficult to teach it to a horse, for he has no understanding of language and lacks the intelligence to learn by watching a trained horse. To teach it requires that a trainer take advantage of every natural instinct of his pupil, and to bend those instincts into entirely new brain patterns.

Since a horse with any instinct to pace is most inclined to use that gait when going downhill, the colt's first lesson in the rack was started at the top of a gently sloping hillside. With the curb reins drawn snug the trainer moved back in the saddle, throwing as much weight as possible onto the colt's hind legs. The pupil was then urged forward with the legs, as if the trot were desired. But the instant he lifted a forefoot, his head was turned a trifle in that direction, and the trainer shifted his weight in the saddle. This threw the colt slightly off balance. Although in the trot he had been taught to move diagonal feet at the same time, he was now unable to do so without the risk of falling.

Balance is tremendously instinctive in a good horse, and it requires no thinking for him to move his legs in whatever manner may be necessary to maintain it. When the colt found himself unable to move the diagonal hind foot without further adding to his imbalance, it was instinctive for him to step forward with the other, as he would naturally do in pacing. But this was not a true pacing step, for both feet on the same side had not moved simultaneously. Even though no thought had been required, it had taken a fraction of a second for the colt to change the pattern of his steps, so the forefoot had left the ground well before the hind was lifted. The necessary pause had been made without intention, the feet would be set down in the same order they had been raised, and the colt would have taken his first step at the new gait.

With the utmost skill and in perfect rhythm, the trainer would continue throwing his pupil off balance from side to side. By the time the bottom of the hill was reached, the colt was usually shuffling in an awkward, confused manner, somewhat between an amble and a hopping trot. But a new man-made gait pattern would already have begun etching itself into his brain.

Day after day and week after week the colt was put through his lesson on the hillside. And with every lesson he gained better control of his balance, his racking gait became smoother, its rhythm more

nearly perfect, and its pattern more deeply etched on his brain. As the gait improved, the trainer shifted his weight and turned the pupil's head less and less. At last he would do neither, but continue to tighten the curb reins a little, and to shake them slightly at the start. By this time the colt had learned to associate the tightening and shaking of the curb reins with the need for regaining his

balance. The moment his mouth felt the vibration of the reins on the curb bit, he fell instinctively into the racking gait, and practice on the hillside was no longer necessary.

The second artificial gait to be taught was usually the stepping pace. This was a variation of the rack, performed in slow motion but with high animation, and with every step precisely and beautifully executed.

The gallop is a horse's natural speed gait. For a horse with high foot action it is a rough, pounding gait, but if the speed is greatly reduced, it becomes a canter, with a smooth, rocking-chair motion. A five-gaited saddler was never allowed to gallop, and never trained at the canter until he had learned all his other gaits thoroughly. Then he was schooled until he could perform the gait at a speed no faster than a man might walk.

The colt had now learned all his gaits, but it was far too early to determine whether or not he would ever become a top-flight saddler. From here on it would depend almost entirely upon his own intelligence, style, showmanship, and sense of artistry — and all of these are inherited traits. Each morning and evening for months — even years — he would be given an hour's exercise to smooth and polish his gaits and manners. He must learn to recognize rein and leg signals given so delicately that a watcher could barely see them, changing instantly to whatever gait was indicated, and at whatever speed was asked.

If the horse had inherited the qualities of greatness, his steps would become a poetry of flowing motion; the beat of his hoofs a cadence of stirring music. His fast rack would be performed at the speed of the hurricane, but with no particle of bounce to the rider, his trot would have the boldness and sparkle of a mountain brook, his stepping pace and canter be so slow and gentle that he could dance them all day long in the shade of an apple tree.

The saddle horse had been developed into a beautifully gaited and mannered animal on the Virginia and Carolina plantations when, in 1775, Daniel Boone blazed the Wilderness Road across the Blue Ridge Mountains and founded the first settlement in Kentucky. Boone's slogan for a happy life was, "a good gun, a good horse, and a good wife." It must also have been the slogan of the thirty pioneers who were his followers, for they took with them their guns, their good wives, and their best saddle horses. These horses were soon known throughout the frontier as the Kentucky saddlers.

With sparkling springs of lime water to build strong bone, and bluegrass to build stout muscles, the Kentucky saddlers improved from generation to generation. But the improvement was never enough to satisfy the Kentucky horsemen. They insisted that their saddle horses be as intelligent, as graceful, and as beautiful as their women. Wherever they went, they searched for sires that might help to beautify and refine their saddlers. Whenever one was found he was bought, regardless of price.

In 1840 Cockspur, a three-year-old saddle stallion, was bought in Virginia and brought to Kentucky. He was as graceful as an antelope, beautiful in conformation and appearance, and his gaits and manners were perfect. Beyond this, he had unusual ability to pass his finest qualities onward, and his daughters became cornerstones in the foundation upon which the American Saddle Horse was built.

By 1850 the pacing horses of Canada had been developed into the finest and fastest on earth. Many excellent Thoroughbreds had been imported to our southern states, and in New York the descendants of Messenger had already laid the foundation for the Standardbred harness racers. In New England the Morgans reigned supreme, dazzling crowds at every fair with their beauty, high-actioned style, and trotting speed.

Kentucky horsemen sought out and brought home many of the finest stallions of each type. Then owners of particularly fine and intelligent mares, graceful and easy-riding at all five gaits, often rode them a hundred miles or more for mating with one of these excellent sires. In this way each of the great stallions founded a widely scattered family of his own.

Doubtless, Cockspur had a greater influence than any other of the imported sires on the new horse breed being founded in Kentucky during the 1800's. But because his finest offspring were daughters, his name has been almost forgotten, while the Denmark and Chief names have become famous.

Denmark was a finely built Thoroughbred race horse who sired many sons, both racers and saddle horses, but only one of them was ever outstanding. In 1850 Denmark was mated with Betsey Harrison, a daughter of Cockspur. Their son, Gaines' Denmark, was the most beautiful and perfectly gaited saddle horse ever to have been foaled in this country. From his father he inherited only speed and fineness of bone, but from his mother he inherited all the marvelous saddle-horse qualities that were Cockspur's, including his wonderful ability to pass those qualities on to future generations. He sired scores of outstanding saddle-horse sons, and established the family that produced Rex McDonald, the first show horse to bring worldwide attention to the breed.

Clark Chief was a huge, rough descendant of Messenger. He had neither refinement nor beauty, but was an amazingly fast trotter, with a bold, free action. Like Denmark, he was mated with a Cockspur mare and she produced his only outstanding son, Harrison Chief. Harrison Chief inherited his father's speed and boldness only, but all the excellent saddle-horse qualities of his mother. With them he established the magnificent Chief family.

By 1891 numerous families of the Kentucky saddle-horses founded by the imported sires had died out because of improper matings. Many, like the Cockspurs, had been absorbed into other families. Some of those that remained had improved remarkably, but had been widely scattered throughout the South and were becoming quite different in type. Each of the better families had its own particular excellence, but no single family combined them all. The Kentucky horsemen realized that if a pure breed were to be established, the blood lines of these excellent families must be drawn together, purified, and protected. In an effort to bring this about they formed an association and established a registry — now the American Saddle Horse Register — for preserving the pedigrees of horses worthy of representing the new breed.

Although the genes (the units of inheritance) are not carried in the blood, this was not known by early horse breeders. They believed the blood of both parents joined to form the new life, and that blood alone controlled heredity. For that reason horse heredity is still spoken of in terms of blood lines. The fusing of blood lines to form a new horse breed is much like the joining of waters to form a great river. Each sire is a spring, and his family the brook that carries his blood onward, mixed with and influenced to a greater or lesser degree by the blood of the mares with whom he is mated. One by one the brooks join, become tributaries, are joined by other tributaries, and flow onward to form a single, unified bloodstream.

Brooks and creeks join by following the route of the least resistance, and the water of the river they form is a composite of every tributary. Near its source a river usually is clear and sparkling, for the water of mountain brooks purifies itself as it leaps and flows over gravelly beds. But in lowlands the creeks move sluggishly, gathering muck from their

banks and carrying it onward to muddy the mainstream of the river. The same is true of a horse
breed.

Although the bloodstream of a pure horse breed
so strongly resembles a river, the blood lines never
join by following the route of least resistance. They
must be drawn together by the careful planning of
many devoted men. The source blood cannot purify
itself as it flows onward. Instead, it will become
muddied and ruined if sluggish blood is allowed to
join it. A clear and sparkling mainstream can be
established only when undesirable qualities are

filtered out of the tributary streams through carefully selected matings. Then the stream must be kept pure by damming out muddy, inferior blood through registration.

Through careful crossbreeding and strict registration requirements, the brooks carrying the blood lines of the best saddle-horse families were joined into tributaries and purified. Within two decades a new and exquisitely beautiful horse breed had been established, but was still divided in three tributaries. These were the Denmark, Chief, and Morgan branches. All three were extremely beautiful, each admired for its outstanding qualities, but each had its weaknesses.

The Denmarks were swan-necked, delicate, and highly refined, with the grace of a ballerina in the performance of their man-made gaits, but were inclined to lack showmanship and boldness. The Chiefs were powerful, bold, and magnificent, with tremendous speed at the rack and trot, but they lacked the easy-riding qualities of the Denmarks and high foot action of the Morgans. The Morgans, though lacking the magnificence of the Chiefs or the grace of the Denmarks, overflowed with that magnetic quality that in people is called personal charm, and in horses is called presence.

The three tributaries were drawn closer together, and the Morgan branch absorbed, through matings of Chief and Denmark sires with Morgan mares. Then the mainstream of all the blood lines was formed when Edna May, the champion Denmark mare, was mated with Bourbon King, the champion Chief stallion. This was the first great marriage — now called the Golden Cross — between the Chief and Denmark families. But Justin Morgan was certainly best man at that wedding, and the Cockspur mares the matrons of honor. Edna May was as much Morgan as Denmark, and Bourbon King — through his mother — nearly as much Morgan as Chief. Both owed their easy-gaited grace to the Cockspurs.

In their son, Edna May's King, the American Saddle Horse, the most beautiful and talented show horse on earth, came into its full splendor. The mainstream first joined in him now flows in the veins of every champion saddler, and its glory brings us out of our seats whenever these peacocks of the show ring strut their stuff and the ringmaster calls *Rack on! Rack on!*

7

The Walking Horse

A SKILLED SCIENTIST may, by combining a few commonly known ingredients, produce a completely unknown and extremely valuable substance. Or, by changing his formula very slightly, he can produce from these same ingredients a wholly different, though new and equally valuable, substance. Kentucky and Tennessee horsemen proved themselves to be skilled scientists by producing two entirely distinct and highly valuable horse breeds from exactly the same foundation stock.

Soon after Daniel Boone led his frontiersmen into Kentucky, other pioneers from Virginia and the Carolinas crossed the mountains and settled in central Tennessee. They, like the Kentuckians, took with them their easy-riding saddle horses. There is little doubt that the horses were very much alike, and remained so for several decades, since the early Tennessee horsemen drew most of their breeding stock from Kentucky.

Among the exceptionally fine sires imported to Kentucky in the early 1800's were Tom Hal and Copperbottom. Both were fast, smooth-gaited Canadian pacers, though having the trotting pattern in their brains. Many horsemen believe their mothers to have been Narragansett Pacer and their fathers Morgan, for both are entered in the Morgan Horse Register.

Tom Hal and Copperbottom were so much alike that one might almost believe them to have been full brothers, though Tom Hal was a blue roan and Copperbottom a red roan. And it is evident that they inherited in exactly the same manner: color and pacing instinct from their mothers; size, muscular strength, gentleness, and presence from their fathers; courage, speed, and beauty from both parents. But most important of all, they had the wonderful Morgan prepotency, enabling them to transmit these characteristics. Their colts were so highly prized as sires and brood mares that they were taken to every part of the American frontier, many of them into Tennessee.

When Tom Hal was thirty-five years old he sired his greatest son, Bald Stockings. This colt became one of the most important sires in both the American Saddle and Tennessee Walking breeds. The motion of his shoulders and hindquarters was as fluid as that of a leopard, and he was the first horse in history to attract national attention for the speed of his walking gait. It was a perfectly square, flat-footed walk, but his extreme suppleness gave it a gliding motion, and made it natural for him to take long, rapid steps. He could travel at eight miles an hour without breaking into a trot, and his hind feet overstepped his fores by nearly twenty inches. In addition, he had inherited the ability to transmit his own finest qualities.

With Bald Stockings the first marked separation in type took place between the horses of Kentucky and Tennessee. This was only natural, for in every part of the world men have developed whatever type of horse would best serve their needs — and enjoyment. Beneath Kentucky and Tennessee there is limestone; it is in the water of the springs and brooks, and in the fiber of the bluegrass. And nothing builds harder bone or stouter muscles in horses than limestone. But, otherwise the land of the two states is quite different, and the needs of the early settlers were equally different.

The Kentucky farms were large, and most of the work was done by field hands and mules. So the Kentuckian's need was for an easy-gaited saddle horse, and he found his greatest enjoyment in horse shows — where he could compete with his neighbor in the beauty and gracefully performed man-made gaits of his saddler. In Tennessee the farms were generally small, the owners and their sons did most of their own field work with horses, and the crops were mostly row crops — cotton, tobacco, and corn. These men had little time for teaching horses the man-made gaits, and little interest in horse shows. Their need was for a docile combination horse, strong enough to pull a plow, steady enough to walk between rows without treading on the crops, gentle and easygoing enough so a woman could ride him with comfort; and he must be handsome enough to double as the family driving horse on Sunday.

In Bald Stockings the Tennesseeans found exactly the qualities they most admired: strength, stamina, a gentle disposition, flashiness of color, and a rapid, easygoing gait that was entirely natural and required no training. They bought and brought home all the Bald Stocking colts who showed a strong inheritance of the gliding, long-striding gait. By mating these colts with their finest mares, the Tennessee farmers fixed the tendency for the running walk in an emerging horse breed.

Each Tennessee community raised horses that were best suited to its own particular needs and enjoyment. Where the farms were small and the farmers did their own field work the horses were large, heavy-boned, and strong-muscled. In communities where the land was rich and large plantations were established, the work was done by mules and field hands, so the owners had little need for a general-purpose horse. By careful matings, these wealthy owners refined their saddle horses, making them higher headed, more slender, finer-boned, and longer-striding in their walking gait. But all these horses had the same general characteristics. As a whole, they were larger and much more heavily muscled than their Kentucky cousins. And instead of being trained to perform the man-made gaits, the tendency for the gliding, running walk had been firmly bred into them.

As, year by year, the Tennessee farmers prospered, more of them could afford to keep a horse that was not needed for field work, and they began taking greater pride in their saddlers. In 1887 the first great Tennessee Fair was held at Nashville. There were Thoroughbred races, harness races, and classes for five-gaited Kentucky Saddlers. But the class that pleased the farmers more than any other was for walking horses. In this class, horses were judged for gentleness, stamina, and beauty — but the greatest credit was given for ability to perform the running walk rapidly, in form, and with an effortless, gliding motion.

The fair of 1887 gave Tennesseeans their first opportunity to exhibit their Walking Horses, and had a tremendous influence on the development of the gait known as the running walk. Every owner of a fine Walking mare coveted the honor of winning first prize at the state fair, and each set about trying to raise a colt that could bring home the blue ribbon. Whenever a colt showed great freedom and ease in his walking stride, coupled with gentleness and other desirable qualities, he was saved as a sire, and the finest mares in his neighborhood were mated with him.

By 1900 there were numerous families of excellent "Plantation Walking Horses" in Tennessee; but each family was somewhat different from any other in size, conformation, and ability to perform the running walk. Some horsemen believe it doubtful that these horses would ever have been developed into a separate, pure, and exquisite breed if it had not been for one single man and one single horse. The man was James Brantley, and the horse was Allan, a registered Standardbred pacer.

Allan was a rather small black stallion, and until he was seventeen years of age showed every indication of disgracing both of the illustrious sires from whom he was descended. On his father's side his pedigree ran straight back through Hambletonian to Messenger. On his mother's side it ran straight back through Black Hawk to Justin Morgan. No finer blood lines could have been combined to produce trotting speed, stamina, and courage. But Allan was a complete contradiction: he was a natural pacer instead of trotter, and before he had been entered in half-a-dozen races he acquired the name of being a cowardly quitter. For the first three quarters of a race he would pace the other starters almost off their feet. Then, coming into the home stretch, he would seem to lose interest, become confused in the rhythm of his stride, and was always last to cross the finish line.

Because of Allan's exceptionally fine breeding, his great beauty, and the extreme length and freedom of his pacing stride, he was tried as a sire of racing horses. But his colts were fully as disappointing as he — worthless for anything but carriage horses.

After Allan's failure as a sire of race horses he was shipped off to Tennessee. It was hoped that there, because of his natural running walk, a good market might be found for him. But, unfortunately, his reputation was already known by Tennessee horsemen. Although they agreed that his running walk was excellent, no one wanted colts by him, and for more than ten years he was traded from owner to owner. In 1900, when good Walking Horse

stallions were bringing a thousand dollars or more, Allan was sold for $97.50. The next year he moved on again in an even-up trade for a black jackass, and on his next move he was traded for an old work mule.

In the spring of 1903, when Allan was seventeen years old, he was offered to James Brantley for $110, a higher price than he had brought in years. Mr. Brantley, like most Tennessee horsemen, had heard of Allan's reputation, but he could not believe that the horse being shown him was actually a quitter. Even at seventeen the little black stallion had the

beauty and animated appearance of a colt. The brightness of his eyes, the alertness of his ears, and his perfectly shaped head showed him to be highly intelligent. The conformation of his body was faultless.

Jim Brantley knew a good horse when he saw one, and he knew that if this little stallion was actually a quitter, there had to be some reason for it in his ancestry. He was so determined to find out what that reason might be that he drove a hundred miles to Louisville to examine the American Trotting Registry. Everything he found in the records confirmed what he believed he had seen in the horse. There had to be some other answer to Allan's failure as a race horse and sire of race horses, and Jim Brantley was determined to find that answer.

When Mr. Brantley returned from Louisville, he drove over and bought the little black stallion nobody wanted. He didn't quibble about the price, but took Allan home, harnessed him to a racing sulky, and drove him out to the track. In half an hour he had his answer: the little horse was no quitter. Just the opposite — he was overanxious to win. It was his will to win that had ruined his reputation. His extreme loose-jointedness, together with long, strong shoulder and thigh muscles, made him an exceptionally long-striding, easygoing, and fast pacer. But when he tried to gather those long muscles for the final sprint, they corded and bound. The harder he tried to turn on the speed, the tighter the muscles cramped and the more they held him back. James Brantley was so delighted with his discovery that, in spite of ridicule by other horse-men, he decided to mate Allan with his own fine mare, Gertrude.

Gertrude was one of the finest Walking Horse mares in Tennessee, and she had reason to be, for there was royal blood in her veins. Her mother, like Allan's, was a fourth-generation Morgan. Her father was Royal Denmark, a fourth-generation descendant of both Gaines' Denmark and Bald Stockings. Gertrude had inherited Bald Stockings' pantherlike walking gait, beautiful roan color, white stocking, and bald face. She was a large, well-muscled, heavily boned mare, with excellent sloping shoulders and a sharply chiseled head that she held high on a graceful neck.

The colt produced by the mating of Allan and

Gertrude was Roan Allen. In him the most excellent qualities of every one of his illustrious forebears seemed to have been concentrated and refined. He had the grace and elegance of the Denmarks, the speed and boldness of the Messengers, the show-manship, high action, and gentle disposition of the Morgans, the stamina and pantherlike motion of the Hals, and the beauty of the Cockspurs, together with the size and gorgeous coloring of Bald Stockings. From all his ancestors combined he inherited the ability to perform every horse gait known to man, making him one of the very few horses ever capable of performing seven gaits in perfect form. But his greatest inheritance was from Justin Morgan alone: the ability to pass on to far distant generations the finest of his own qualities.

Roan Allen was a red roan, fifteen hands and three inches tall, with a broad white strip in his face, high white stockings on his hind legs, and socks on his fores. His tail, like his mane, was long and flaxen, and he carried it proudly. Horsemen who knew him said the conformation of his body was the nearest to perfection they had ever seen. His back was short, his hip coupling strong, his thighs, forearms, and shoulders were heavily muscled. He was deep in the chest and well-sprung in the ribs; with a magnificent head held erect on a long and graceful, though strongly muscled neck. There can be little wonder that Tennessee horsemen chose him as the ideal toward which a new and pure breed of horses would be developed.

In Roan Allen's day Walking Horses were unknown outside Tennessee, and there were few competitions elsewhere in which they could be entered, but that made little difference to Jim Brantley. He entered Roan Allen in every horse show throughout the state; in walking, light-harness, three-gaited, and five-gaited classes — and he won wherever he was shown. At the running walk his stride was so long that his hind feet overstepped his fores by more than three feet. He performed the gait flat-footed and in perfect four-beat rhythm, but with a gliding, catlike motion so rapid that he could travel at better than ten miles an hour. His trot was perfectly square, bold, high-actioned, and fast. He could scorch the track with the speed of his pacing gait and rack a hole in the wind, but his canter and slow gait were no faster than a dog will trot — and both were poems of gentle rhythm and grace.

When Roan Allen was foaled, many Tennessee horsemen refused to credit his father with any of his excellence. Because the colt was colored like his mother, and had the frame and conformation of a Walking Horse, they claimed that he had inherited every one of his fine qualities from Gertrude, and nothing from the little black stallion who had for seventeen years proved himself to be a failure. When, soon after, Allan sired Hunter's Allen, foaled by a Copperbottom mare, these same horsemen were the first to shout his praise. Overnight Allan became the most famous stallion in Tennessee. There was no horseman in the state who would not have traded a whole herd of mules for him, and every owner of an exceptionally fine Walking mare clamored to mate her with the "wonder horse."

Although Hunter's Allen lacked the multiple-gaitedness and gorgeous coloring of his roan half brother, his running walk was fully as good. He was a magnificent show horse: golden chestnut, with marvelous presence, showmanship, and style. During his long show-ring career he won hundreds of blue ribbons, and his courage was unconquerable. In his twentieth year he was entered in the Bedford County Fair, in the best class of Walking Horse stallions ever to have been gathered in the state. From the moment he stepped into the arena he seemed to sense the keenness of the competition, and to realize that he might be considered an old has-been among a great class of stallions in their prime. Horsemen who saw the show say that no horse ever put on a braver performance. The records show that, "Hunter's Allen walked up a storm," and he carried off the championship.

The prepotency of old Justin Morgan was strong in both these great sons of little black Allan. Roan Allen's ability to pass on his most excellent qualities was amazing. Nearly half a century after his birth,

every one of the twenty-five top-ranked stallions listed in the Tennessee Walking Horse Register were his male-line descendants. The offspring of Hunter's Allen, though not so excellent, won the Walking Horse stakes at the Tennessee State Fair in nine of the fourteen contests held between 1920 and 1933.

After Roan Allen and Hunter's Allen had brought him fame, Allan was mated with only the finest Walking mares — mares in whose veins flowed the blood of all the fine horses who had founded the American Saddle Horse breed. When Allan brought to these matings the concentrated blood of the Morgans and Messengers a new and wonderful breed of horses came into being. But if it had not been for James Brantley's faith in an unwanted little black stallion there would probably have been no new breed — and Allan would have died a failure rather than a wonder horse.

By the time Roan Allen and Hunter's Allen reached maturity they had several hundred half brothers and half sisters in central Tennessee — each marked with Allan's loose-jointed walking gait, his speed in performing it, his gentle disposition, his beauty, and his showmanship. But Allan had been well past his prime when James Brantley discovered him. None of his later colts ever quite equaled his first two famous sons, and they had barely reached full maturity when, in 1910, the little black stallion died. But only a part of him died, for in those two sons he had left the potency to carry on the perfecting of the new breed.

In 1935 the Tennessee Walking Horse Breeders' Association was formed, held its first meeting, established a registry, and passed resolutions for unifying and perfecting a pure and unique breed. So well did they carry out their resolutions that within fifteen years the families had been welded into a completely unified type, and the United States Government formally recognized the Tennessee Walking Horse as a pure and separate breed. Beyond this, the breed — almost unknown outside its native state in 1935 — had become so popular throughout the nation that more than forty thousand purebred Walkers had been produced, registered, and sold.

Few horses of any breed can match the Tennessee Walker as a pleasure horse. His gaits — the walk, the running walk, and rocking-chair canter — are all natural to him, so he needs no expert training. His disposition is so gentle that any woman or child can handle and ride him safely under any condition. The smoothness of his flowing motion makes riding him a joy, and his beauty is dazzling as he glides along a woodland trail. In the show ring he has won himself a warm spot in the hearts of all horse lovers. He may not bring us out of our seats, as the American Saddler — the peacock of the show ring — does with the wild glory of his whirlwind rack, but few can watch him slip along, head bobbing gaily, without longing to put an arm around his neck and a leg across his back.

8

Stymie — Just Common Folks

ALTHOUGH the Thoroughbred race horse was originated in England, the horsemen of this country have improved and developed the breed to such an extent that American horses now hold ninety per cent of all the world's speed records. The greatest of them all was Man o' War. He and his ancestors were the aristocrats of American Thoroughbred royalty. Their speed and determination to win were so great that no jockey could hold them back in the driving finish of a race, and some of them were so hot-blooded as to be nearly unmanageable.

There was nothing regal about Stymie, even though both his grandmothers were daughters of Man o' War. He wasn't even born in the bluegrass country, but on the King ranch in Texas. And instead of being hot-blooded and unmanageable, he was as friendly and gentle as a puppy. When the other colts raced at play in the pasture, Stymie was content to string along at the tail end, or stay behind and visit with the mares. When a New York sports reporter looked him over he wrote, "Stymie is just common folks — the most average horse you ever saw. Not tall, not short, not long, not close coupled. Good bone, good muscle, good chest — nothing outstanding, nothing poor."

In his training as a yearling, Stymie was a sad disappointment. The only good quality he appeared to have inherited from his famous ancestors was Man o' War's long, powerful stride, but he lacked drive and determination to win, so the stride was worthless to him. There was hardly a colt on the King ranch that couldn't outrun him at a half mile.

As a two-year-old Stymie was shipped North and entered in a $2500 claiming race. The odds were thirty-one to one against him, and he proved them to be about right. In such a race any other owner could have claimed him for $2500, but no one wanted him that badly. Neither did the owners of the King ranch, so he was entered in races where the claiming price — and the speed of the other colts — was less, but Stymie showed no interest in racing. With each loss he was entered in lower classes, until he was running in $1500 claiming races — almost the bottom rung on the ladder; but still he didn't win.

In the middle of the season Stymie was claimed by Hirsch Jacobs for $1500, although he had run a dozen races and never come close to winning. Under his new owner he did better, ending the season with a record of twenty-eight races run — four won, second place eight times, and third four times.

Considering the class of competition, the record could hardly be called brilliant, yet Hirsch Jacobs believed he saw a hint of greatness in the colt. Stymie had not only shown determination and drive in the finish of his last few races, but had come through a rugged season in perfect condition. Racing puts a tremendous strain on a horse, and before running a score of races many Thoroughbreds break down because of some weakness in their makeup — hoofs, ankles, or cannon bones too frail to hold up under the terrific pounding; tendons that snap or bow at high tension, unsound wind, or nerves that cannot stand the excitement. Some of the greatest race horses of all time — including Man o' War — never ran as many as twenty-eight races in their entire careers.

Usually a colt that has had a hard season is given a long winter's rest, where he can fill out from a stripling into a full-bodied horse, and be brought to the peak of condition for the great three-year-old classics. Stymie was given no such rest. In the first place he had never shown enough speed to indicate that he would have the slightest chance in the classics. In the second place he showed no need of rest, so Hirsch Jacobs shipped him straight to Florida for the winter campaign.

Because Stymie had won or placed second in his last few races, he was moved into faster company when he reached Florida. Although he showed improvement with every race, the best he could do was to run second or third. He was always slow in getting into full stride, at the half-mile post the faster-starting colts had left him far behind, and he could never make up the lost ground before they reached the finish wire.

Stymie had become a three-year-old before he won his first race in fast company. With a driving finish down the home stretch he nosed out the highly regarded Olympic Zenith in a race at a mile and seventy yards. That race was a turning point in Stymie's life, for it showed clearly that if given enough distance he could make up for his lack of speed through sheer courage and stamina.

After a good showing in the Wood Memorial race Stymie was entered in the mile-and-three-quarter Gallant Fox Handicap — his first race against top-notch competition. By the time three quarters of the race had been run he was trailing far back at the tail end, looking as if he were completely out-

classed. Then, at the far turn, his head came up and his ears pricked forward, almost as though he sensed that the highly touted horses running away from him might be tiring. In a burst of speed such as he had never before shown, he made his bid and overhauled the tiring laggards as they rounded the end of the oval.

As Stymie turned into the stretch he was in full flight, but only those who had seen Man o' War run — more than twenty years before — would have believed he was putting out his best effort. When in a driving burst of speed, practically all Thorough-

breds lower their necks, thrust their muzzles out, and lay their ears back, but the faster Stymie ran the higher and more proudly he held his head. Head high and chestnut mane whipping back like a flag in a hurricane, he called on a reserve of power that no other horse in the race could match. One by one he passed horses that had been rated far above him; but he had been too late in making his bid. The best he could do was to take third place, though he had gained on the winners right up to the wire.

During the rest of his three-year-old season Stymie won no important races, but threw away a couple that he should have won, and all because of a peculiar quirk in his nature. Right from the day he was born he had shown that he was just common folks, loved company, and was lonesome without it. In these races his rider had put him eight or ten lengths in the lead before the far turn was reached. But Stymie was lonesome out there all alone, so he paid no attention to the whip and dropped back to run with the pack, while some poorer horse went on to win. Even with these losses he picked up enough second and third places to bring his winnings for two years up to $58,000. Although the sum was not bad for a colt who had sold in the middle of his first season for $1500, it was far from impressive, for he had run in fifty races to win it. Pavot, a two-year-old colt who had run only eight races, had won nearly $180,000.

All hope that Stymie might win fame or a great amount of money seemed gone. Fame and big purses are won in the Kentucky Derby, Preakness, Belmont Stakes, and other such famous races, but these are for three-year-olds only. Few Thoroughbreds past that age have ever won either fame or fortune, for they can then be won only in handicap or stake races — and for those a horse must have more than speed alone; he must also have indomitable courage, an unquenchable will to win, and the strength and stamina to run long distances while carrying a heavy load.

Handicap races are just what the name indicates. The ideal race would be one in which all the horses were exactly equal in both speed and endurance. But this is impossible, for a horse's speed and endurance depend greatly upon his condition at the time of the race and the distance to be run. Handicapping is a system of adjusting the speed that may be expected from each horse, based upon his recent performances, and he is slowed down about two lengths to the mile by each one-pound lead plate the handicapper requires him to carry in his saddle pad.

Stymie's poor showing as a three-year-old was in his favor when he returned to the track as a handicap horse in the spring of 1945. He was given light weight to carry in his first two races, and did well, winning one and being beaten by a nose in the other. His first important race that season was the Grey Lag Handicap, in which he was given average weight to carry and was ridden by Bobby Permane.

From past performances it was evident to Stymie's trainer that the highheaded chestnut had his own ideas about the way a race should be run, and that he could do his best only if he thought he was doing the right thing at the right time. When the horses went to the post for the Grey Lag Handicap the trainer instructed Bobby Permane to let Stymie run his own race. As he had done in the Gallant Fox, he got away to a slow start. Until he reached the far end of the back stretch he seemed content to gallop along effortlessly behind the field. But his ears were pricked forward, his eyes sparkled, and he kept watch of the front-runners as they pulled away from the pack — almost as though he were judging exactly how much lead he might allow them and still beat them to the wire. As they leaned into the far turn Stymie's head came up, he lengthened his powerful stride, and made his bid without the slightest urging from Bobby Permane.

Gaining speed at every leap, Stymie overhauled the laggards and turned into the home stretch literally flying — head high, mane and tail streaming back in the breeze, and leaping better than twenty-five feet at every stride. But the front-runners were already far down the stretch, with the favorite, Alex Barth, well out in front.

No one can say whether it was judgment or inherited instinct that told Stymie when to make his bid. Whichever it might have been, he had made it at exactly the right instant. While horses whose past performances rated them far above him tired and faltered in their drive for the wire, Stymie streaked past them as fresh as when he had come from the stable. He was still pulling away when he led Alex Barth under the wire, winner by half a length.

That was Stymie's first win as a stake racer — though far from his last — and he had done it all by himself. It might almost seem that he had deliberately waited until the last possible moment before making his bid, so as to save himself the task he hated — that of running alone at the front of the pack. Once Stymie had discovered the thrill of driving from far behind and winning, he reveled in it, but to him there was evidently no sense in pouring on speed when he was already out in front.

Stymie was always a slow starter. His only hope was to depend upon courage, stamina, and a reserve of power that made it possible for him to run his best at a time when his faster rivals were tiring. A mile and a quarter was the very shortest distance that would let him take advantage of these qualities. Most of the stake races that offered large purses were at about that distance, and many of the speedsters with whom he must compete could run it without tiring badly. Among the best of them were Devil Diver, First Fiddle, Pavot, Alex Barth, and Olympic Zenith.

Following Stymie's surprise winning of the Grey Lag Handicap he was entered in the rich Suburban

Handicap, which paid nearly $40,000 to the winner. Again he made a gallant bid and overhauled the field in a dazzling stretch drive, but the distance was only a mile and a quarter, so Devil Diver beat him to the wire. The story was the same in the Queens County Handicap, but this time it was Olympic Zenith, carrying a lighter load, that he was unable to overtake. He more than evened the score by beating them soundly in winning the longer Brooklyn Handicap, the Butler Handicap, and the Saratoga Cup, although carrying greater weight.

One of the most coveted prizes in stake racing is the winning of the Jockey Club Gold Cup. The two-mile distance was enough to give Stymie full advantage of his stamina, and too great for such speedsters as Devil Diver, First Fiddle, or Pavot to run without tiring. Most horsemen believed that Stymie couldn't possibly be beaten, but he was. It was not by a superior horse, but by one of the most brilliant jockeys this country has ever known.

Eddie Arcaro rode Pavot in this race and Basil James rode Stymie. It proved to be a contest between jockeys rather than horses. Pavot was a top-notch sprinter. The previous year he had been the two-year-old champion, winning all eight races in which he was entered and earning more money than any other horse in the country. He was a very fast starter and, in a race of a mile or less, could run the slow-starting Stymie into the ground. But he lacked the chestnut's tremendous endurance, and didn't have an outside chance with him in a race of a mile and a half or more. No one knew this better than Eddie Arcaro, and he knew something that Basil James didn't know — Stymie's hatred for running all alone in front of the pack.

Before every important race the trainer and jockey of each horse plan their strategy carefully, based upon what may be expected of every other horse in the race. Although it was generally conceded that Stymie would win the Jockey Club Gold Cup, the purse for second place was larger than the winner's share in many other races, so most of the plans were made for winning that prize — and they were laid around Eddie Arcaro and Pavot. Pavot was unquestionably the fastest horse in the race, and it was fully expected that Arcaro would set the early pace with him, trying to gain enough lead so that only Stymie could overtake him before reaching the finish wire. With this in mind, the other jockeys planned to hang back of Arcaro, keeping just close enough to be in position for making their bids when Pavot showed his first signs of tiring.

When the barrier was sprung the horses leaped away in an almost even row. Each jockey's mind — with the exception of Basil James's and Eddie Arcaro's — was set on the position he would try to take behind Pavot. For Basil, there was no need of jockeying for position. All that seemed necessary during the first mile and a half was to keep Stymie swinging along in his usual long-striding gallop, regardless of position. Then, as the other horses began to tire, he would make his bid, pass them in the home stretch as though they were hobbled, and win by as many lengths as he chose.

Before the horses were ten lengths away from the barrier the whole race was in confusion. Contrary to all expectations, Arcaro had failed to gain the rail and shoot Pavot out in front. Instead, he was obviously holding the colt back. Until he took the lead there seemed nothing for the other jockeys to do but to pull their mounts up and take the positions they had originally planned on. But Eddie didn't turn Pavot loose. During the first quarter mile he held him down almost to the speed of a trotting horse — and the confusion grew. Eddie Arcaro was recognized as one of the keenest judges of pace in the horse-racing business, and none of the other boys was willing to challenge his judgment. He must think the pace he was setting to be as fast as was prudent in so long a race, so they continued to hang behind him.

All the excitement about position and pace was of no interest to Basil James. He kept Stymie swinging along at the effortless pace he had always taken in the early stages of his races. But before the halfway pole was reached he found himself well out in front of the pack. Now it was Stymie's turn to become confused. He wasn't used to being out in front at this stage in a race, and he didn't like it. He wanted to be back there with the rest of the fellows — where he'd have a little company and could see what was going on — so he paid no attention to Basil's whip, and slowed down to let the others catch up with him.

All through the back stretch Arcaro held Pavot to a pace that any good Thoroughbred could have kept up for several miles without tiring. Behind him the other jockeys held their positions, trying to figure out what Eddie was up to. By the time they discovered the answer it was too late. With his uncanny sense of pace, together with a little psychology and his knowledge of Stymie's hatred for running in front, Eddie Arcaro had turned a distance race into a sprint — and he was mounted on one of the fastest sprinters of the season. When, at last, he turned the still-fresh Pavot loose, Stymie was too bemused to put up a brilliant stretch drive. He finished a poor third, five lengths behind Pavot.

Carrying top weight, Stymie won both the Westchester Stake and Continental Handicap, but in the Pimlico Special the distance was only one and three-sixteenths miles, and the weight was too great for so short a run. Again he finished third — this time behind Devil Diver and First Fiddle. In the Riggs Handicap he evened the score with a tremendous stretch drive, caught First Fiddle in the last few strides, and beat him under the wire by half a length.

Only one horse in thousands could have stood up to the grueling schedule of races that Stymie had run in his four-year-old season, but when he came out of the Riggs Handicap he was just rounding into the peak of condition. And, as Joe Palmer, the famous racing writer for the New York *Herald Tribune,* put it, "When Stymie comes to the peak of condition, he exudes vitality so you expect to hear it crackle. He comes to a hard, lean fitness that you seldom see in domestic animals . . . This is when, as Hirsch Jacobs says, he gets 'rough.' It isn't temper or mean-ness. He just gets so full of himself that he wants things to happen."

In the last race of Stymie's 1945 season, the Pim-lico Cup, he had a chance to show every atom of the stuff of which he was made — and that he hadn't forgotten the crafty trick Eddie Arcaro had played on him. The Pimlico Cup is the longest Thorough-bred classic run in this country — two and a half miles. Under the best of conditions it is an exhaust-ing test of stamina and fitness, but on the day of the 1945 running it was a nightmare. There had been a steady, soaking rain, and the Pimlico track was hoof deep with sticky mud. To make it worse, the handicapper had assigned Stymie a load of 128 pounds before it was known that the track would be

muddy. Then too, besides racing against topnotch horses with lighter loads, he would be up against Pot o' Luck, one of the best mudders and distance runners of his time.

Bobby Permane was again in the saddle when the barrier was sprung for the cup race, and Stymie was bubbling over with eagerness to run. With two and a half miles of heavy going ahead, Bobby held him back, letting the rest of the field take the lead and set the pace. Pot o' Luck's jockey pulled up too, and hung close at Stymie's heels. This was no speed-burning race, but one of power and endurance —

and Pot o' Luck had never yet met a horse that could outstay him. They'd hang behind Stymie till he became leg weary, then overpower him in the run to the finish wire.

For two full miles the race slogged on monotonously. Pot o' Luck still clung to Stymie's heels, the only break in the monotony was when some exhausted front-runner dropped back as was expected, and the fans in the grandstand began to lose interest. Then, in the middle of the back stretch, Bobby Permane suddenly turned Stymie loose. One might have thought he had turned a switch that shot a charge of electricity into every fan in the grandstand. Instantly they were on their feet, shrieking and yelling like fiends. And they had plenty to yell about.

The moment the reins slackened Stymie's head flew up, and he leaped away as if he had been shot from a catapult. His drive was so instantaneous and overpowering that it left Pot o' Luck dazed in his tracks. Within barely a hundred yards Stymie had passed the entire field and was out in front alone. But this time there was no slowing down to let the other fellows catch up — one licking through that sort of foolishness was enough.

With the crowd shrieking in a frenzy of excitement, the highheaded, mud-spattered great-grandson of Man o' War thundered around the near turn and into the home stretch. With that crowd cheering him on he had no need for the stimulant of another horse out in front of him, and like any great showman, he responded with the very best he had. Widening the distance between himself and the field at every powerful stride, he carried his 128-pound load proudly past the grandstand and under the wire, winner by a full eight lengths.

That was not only the greatest race Stymie had ever run but one of the greatest ever run in Maryland. And it was not only the Maryland fans who took him to their hearts but the horse lovers of the entire nation. When his saddle was hung up and he went home for a well-earned winter's rest he was the most popular race horse in America.

Stymie holds a distinction that is shared by no other horse in the history of Thoroughbred racing. Nearly every race he ran was an almost exact parallel of his racing career as a whole. He was a slow starter, always outrun in the early stages of a race, and appearing to be completely outclassed. In the back stretch, where the fans watch eagerly for early indications of a winner, Stymie was unimpressive — content to gallop with the also-rans, or to string along behind them. Then, at the far turn, when the eyes of the fans were focused on the favorites, when lesser horses were beginning to falter, and when most of the jockeys had forgotten he was even in the race, Stymie would make his bid. Coming on from far back in a late but overwhelming drive, he would pass the also-rans before reaching the near turn. Then, gaining speed and power at every stride, he would wage his duel with the favorites in the home stretch. And, if the race were long enough, he would overtake and beat the best of them to the wire.

In the first half of Stymie's two-year-old season he was a complete failure, and in spite of his royal ancestry he showed no indication that he would ever become a successful race horse. A racing colt's three-year-old season is the back stretch of his career. It is then that he usually shows whether or not he has the ability to pull away from the pack and gain a position which will put him in contention for greatness. Some colts are such fast starters and magnificent stretch-runners that they win greatness as three-year-olds; Man o' War won immortality. Stymie's showing was so poor that racing enthusiasts lost sight of him, their attention focused on Whirl-away, Count Fleet, and Pensive. It was not until he was a four-year-old — the far turn in a race horse's career — that, from far back, he made his bid for greatness. Then, as in most of the races he ran that year, his drive was so overpowering that it swept him past the field and into a stretch battle for honors with the finest horses of his time.

Just as Stymie had gained power and speed in the later stages of his races, he gained them in the later years of his career. When he returned to the track for his five-year-old season he was unquestionably one of the best-conditioned, sturdiest, and finest stake racers seen on the American tracks in a decade. The handicappers soon set about adding enough lead to his saddle pad so that he couldn't outdistance the less rugged competition. It slowed him down, but not enough to keep him away from the big purses, for the load he was required to carry was no match for his stamina, courage, and determination. He was entered in twenty of the richest stake races in the East, won eight of them, and failed to place in only one. At the end of the season he had not only won the admiration of horsemen and racing fans throughout the entire country; he had won purses enough to bring his life's winnings above the half-million-dollar mark.

Although Stymie won the admiration of the country's racing enthusiasts in 1946, he was not the most popular race horse of that season. That honor went to Assault, one of the eight horses in history ever to win the Triple Crown: the Kentucky Derby, Preakness, and Belmont Stakes. Strangely enough, Assault, like Stymie, was born on the King ranch, and Assault was the one horse who threatened to snatch Stymie's claim to greatness away from him.

In horse racing as in human athletics, advancing age, stiffening muscles, diminishing vitality, and injuries are the most severe handicappers. Most horses at the age of six years, like most men at the age of thirty, are past their prime — if not long since broken down and out of competition. There are few Ray Robinsons, Archie Moores, Babe Ruths — or Stymies. When, in 1947, he came up for his six-year-old season he was fairly crackling with vitality, and as lean and hard-muscled as a grey-hound. From his eagerness to run, one might have thought he realized as fully as Hirsch Jacobs did that if he were ever to attain greatness, to become champion money winner in racing history, he must do it that season.

But if ever a horse seemed to be stymied in any such an attempt, Stymie was the one. Assault was now a four-year-old and had joined the stake-racing ranks. In the previous season alone he had won $424,195. Beyond that, Stymie had never in his life seen a day when he could match such dazzling speed as Assault's. If he were to win over his King-ranch cousin he would have to do it through sheer courage, stamina, and a reserve of vitality such as had never before been possessed by any horse.

The seesaw battle of 1947 between the two great King-ranch rivals is one of the most thrilling stories in American Thoroughbred racing. In the Grey Lag Handicap, at a mile and three-sixteenths, Assault ran away from Stymie and won easily. Then Stymie streaked under the wire first to win the Metropolitan. In his next start, the Brooklyn Handicap, Assault outran him to the wire and he had

to settle for second place. Then Stymie won the Questionnaire Handicap, with another win in the Sussex after only a week's rest. In these two wins he earned enough to make him the world's greatest money winner, but Assault won again before another week was past, taking Stymie's championship away from him.

The showdown came in the $100,000 Empire Gold Cup race, and it was generally conceded that one or the other of the two great rivals would win it. At the start Stymie let the speedsters streak on ahead, while he settled into the long-striding, rhythmic pace he always held in the early part of a race. His Nemesis, Eddie Arcaro, was on Assault and held him back to the same pace, evidently convinced that he could repeat the trick he had played when Pavot beat Stymie in the Jockey Club Gold Cup.

Neither horse's jockey had much respect for the rest of the field, and let Natchez steal a very long lead in the back stretch. With only three-eighths of a mile left in the race, Natchez's lead looked dangerous to Arcaro, so he made a slashing bid with Assault.

Every eye in the grandstand was on Assault as

Arcaro brought him up in a dizzying rush to overtake Natchez. But Natchez had plenty left with
which to stave off the challenge. Before his chal-
lenger could entirely close the gap, he put on a
terrific burst of speed and led Assault into the home
stretch winging. Stymie was completely forgotten
as the crowd leaped to its feet, cheering on Natchez,
the outsider. And Natchez responded to their
cheers. Hugging close to the rail, his ears tight
against his outstretched neck, he literally stormed
down the stretch, not only standing off Assault's
challenge but pulling away from him. Amazed and
delighted by the unexpected upset, the fans cheered
wildly as, fifty feet from the wire, Natchez seemed
to be the certain winner.

Then, as if coming out of nowhere, Stymie flashed
by on the outside, his flying mane and tail giving
him the appearance of being air-borne. Stymie's hurricane finish was so awe-inspiring that for a moment
the crowd stood spellbound, unable to believe what
it had seen. Then it went nearly insane. With a
shout that shook the stands, fans and horsemen alike
cheered the highheaded chestnut that would not be
robbed of his greatness. When Stymie cantered

back to the winner's circle he was again the champion, the greatest money winner in racing history. And more too, he was again the most popular horse in America.

The mark of true greatness in either man or horse is his ability to rise above himself when confronted with a crisis: to discover within himself a hidden reserve of power that makes it possible for him to perform the seemingly impossible. Never before had Stymie even approached the blinding speed that swept him past Assault and Natchez to win the Empire Gold Cup, but greatness was in him and it responded when he was faced with the gravest crisis of his lifetime. That was the peak of Stymie's brilliant career. He never again attained such unbelievable speed — but he never again was confronted with a crisis. During the remainder of his racing career no horse was ever able to challenge his championship.

Glorious and awe-inspiring as Stymie's finish of the Empire Gold Cup race had been, it was possibly not his most spectacular. He was a showman of uncanny talent and, no matter how dull the script of a show, he could convert the action into stirring drama. He proved it at Boston soon after his Empire victory.

Stymie had never raced at Boston, but the clamor of the fans there was so great that he was entered in the Massachusetts Handicap at Suffolk Downs. And, although there were some excellent horses in the race, the fans flocked to bet their money on Stymie, making him the odds-on favorite.

At the start, and on around the clubhouse turn, Stymie appeared to take no interest in the race, but trailed along behind as if he were following a pack of hounds in a hunt. At the half-mile post he was thirty lengths behind the leaders, obviously out of the race. The disappointed fans were already reaching into pockets for their mutuel tickets, ready to tear them up in disgust, when Stymie tossed his head higher. Showman that he was, he had hung back until the very last instant that was safe before making his drive for the wire. He'd come there to put on a show for his Boston fans, and they'd bet their money on him. He had no idea of letting them down, but he couldn't very well put on a dramatic show for them until he had the stage properly set.

Stymie's drive to the wire was nothing short of

electrifying, and he had judged the ability of the horses in front of him with unbelievable accuracy. While the fans neared the edge of insanity in their excitement, he overtook and passed the main body of the field on the turn. With his high head and streaming mane giving him more the appearance of flying than running, he skimmed down the home stretch, sailed past the front-runners as though they were wading in deep mud, and streaked under the wire to win amid the wildest cheering Suffolk Downs had ever heard.

Stymie raced one more season — though never again so brilliantly as in the Empire Cup and Massachusetts Handicap — swelled his earnings to $918,485, and retired the money-winning champion of the world. But he remained common folks throughout his entire career. Nature had failed to endow him with the regal beauty, overwhelming power, and matchless speed of Man o' War.

While Count Fleet, Assault, and Citation flashed like meteors across the sky of the racing world Stymie galloped along below, unable to match either their speed or brilliance. Each of them was a Triple Crown winner, each in his turn was top-money winner of the year, and each established new speed records. Stymie, limited by lack of early speed, could attain no single one of these honors. But what he lacked in speed he made up for in courage, endurance, stamina, and his wonderful ability to rise above his limitations when faced by seemingly insurmountable odds. His was no meteor flight to glory; he had to win his championship the hard way, hammering it out over six of the most rugged campaigns any horse ever endured, and running 142 miles in 131 races — a record all three of his famous rivals combined could not begin to match.

Count Fleet raced only as a two- and three-year-old, then had to be retired with injuries that would not respond to treatment. Assault ran less than half so many races as Stymie and passed his prime much earlier. Citation reached his peak at three, was sidelined with injuries when four, and ran in only sixteen races thereafter. But when, at the end of his sixth racing season, indestructible Stymie was retired to become a successful sire, he was sound as a silver dollar, and as brimming over with vitality as a yearling.

Bibliography

HORSES by George Gaylord Simpson (New York: Oxford, 1951)

THE HORSE IN MOTION by J. D. B. Stillman (Boston: Osgood, 1882)

THOROUGHBRED RACING STOCK by Lady Wentworth (New York: Scribner, 1938)

THE INFLUENCE OF RACING AND THE THOROUGHBRED HORSE ON LIGHT HORSE BREEDING by William Scarth Dixon (New York: Dingwall-Rock, Ltd., 1924)

ENGLISH RACER AND SADDLE-HORSE by Thomas Hookham (London: Roworth, 1835)

THE BREEDERS' GAZETTE, Vols. I and II, published by J. H. Senders & Co., Chicago, 1882.

A STUDY OF RURAL SOCIETY by J. H. Koll and Edmund deS. Brunner (Boston: Houghton Mifflin, 1940)

THE MORGAN HORSE REGISTER, published at 90 Broad Street, New York City.

FAMOUS SADDLE HORSES by Emily E. Scharf (Louisville, Ky.: Standard Printing Co., Inc., 1931). *Farmers' Home Journal*

DRIVERS UP by Dwight Akers (New York: Putnam, 1947)

THE HORSE OF THE AMERICAS by Robert M. Denhardt (Norman: Univ. of Okla. Press, 1947)

CAVALCADE OF AMERICAN HORSES by Pers Crowell (New York: McGraw-Hill, 1951)

THE HORSEMAN'S ENCYCLOPEDIA by Margaret Cabell Self (New York: Barnes, 1946)

THE HORSE by D. J. Kays (New York: Barnes, 1953)

THIS WAS RACING by Joe H. Palmer (New York: Barnes, 1953)

THE MUSTANGS by J. Frank Dobie (Boston: Little, Brown, 1952)

HORSES AND AMERICANS by Phil Stong (Garden City, N.Y.: Garden City Pub. Co., 1946)

THE INDIAN AND THE HORSE by Frank Gilbert Row (Norman: Univ. of Okla. Press, 1955)

THE AMERICAN TROTTER by John Hervey (New York: Coward-McCann, 1947)

THE AMERICAN RACING MANUAL (New York: Triangle Publications). *Daily Racing Form*

COMPLETE BOOK OF HORSES by Howard J. Lewis (New York: Random House, 1957)

INDEX